Making Creative Baskets

Making Creative Baskets

Alternative Materials ■ Simple Techniques

Jane LaFerla

LARK BOOKS

A Division of Sterling Publishing Co., Inc.
New York

Art Direction: Kathleen Holmes
Photography: Evan Bracken
Illustrations: Hannes Charen

Library of Congress Cataloging-in-Publication Data
Available

10 9 8 7 6 5 4 3 2 1

Published by Lark Books, a division of
Sterling Publishing Co., Inc.
387 Park Avenue South, New York, N.Y. 10016

First Paperback Edition 2002
© 2000, Lark Books

Distributed in Canada by Sterling Publishing,
c/o Canadian Manda Group, One Atlantic Ave., Suite 105
Toronto, Ontario, Canada M6K 3E7

Distributed in the U.K. by:
Guild of Master Craftsman Publications Ltd.
Castle Place, 166 High Street Lewes East Sussex, England BN7 1XU
Tel: (+ 44) 1273 477374 Fax: (+ 44) 1273 478606
Email: pubs@thegmcgroup.com, Web: www.gmcpublications.com

Distributed in Australia by Capricorn Link (Australia) Pty Ltd., P.O. Box 704, Windsor, NSW 2756 Australia

If you have questions or comments about this book, please contact:
Lark Books
67 Broadway
Asheville, NC 28801
(828) 236-9730

Printed in China

ISBN 1-57990-151-4 (hbk) ISBN 1-57990-382-7 (pbk)

Acknowledgments

I would like to thank the project designers and gallery artists who contributed to this book. This endeavor would not be possible without their interest, enthusiasm, and talents. Special thanks to Billie Ruth Sudduth for generously sharing her network, also to Rob Dobson, and Michael Davis. For her abundant creativity and support, extra thanks to Dyan Mai Peterson. Thanks also to Ashely Siegel for the generous use of her home. At Lark, thanks to Hannes Charen for his illustrations and Kathy Holmes for her art direction.

Table of Contents

Baskets from New Materials

Ask friends to describe their favorite basket, and you'll get an array of answers ranging from a wastebasket to the collectible work of a noted artisan. Whether they are large or small, intricately woven or simply made, baskets continue to be a part of our everyday lives—just as they have been for thousands of years.

Baskets are one of the few utilitarian items that developed in similar form throughout all cultures, predating pottery and woven cloth. By weaving or lashing together the pliable plant matter at hand, our ancestors were able to fashion containers for gathering and storing food and transporting other items.

Over the centuries, basket-making techniques have changed very little. Look at any large display of baskets, and you can easily classify them according to the basic techniques of weaving, plaiting, twining, or coiling. What continues to change is the wide variety of new materials contemporary basket makers are using within the craft. Like the earliest basket makers, the new basket makers are harvesting the available materials of our time and transforming them into works of art.

Ed Rossbach, noted fiber artist, defined and inspired the movement of using new materials for basket making. In his book, *The New Basketry*, published in 1976, Rossbach traced the evolution of this exploration to the early "fiberworkers" of the 1950s who began experimenting with off-loom weaving. Rossbach's innovative baskets combine craftsmanship with artistic vision, elevating the materials and forms to thought-provoking sculptures. His work continues to inspire and enlighten new generations.

Twenty-four talented designers created the projects for this book. Some have been using new materials for years, some were intrigued by the opportunity to experiment with unfamiliar mediums, and all created wonderful projects for you to make.

Though you may catch a fleeting glimpse of rush or reed, the majority of materials used to create the baskets are nontraditional, such as paper, cardboard, plastic, and wire. You may even see several projects or gallery pieces that stretch your personal definition of basket—and that is exactly why they are in this book.

How to Use This Book

Even if you've never made a basket before, you'll find illustrated sections explaining the basic techniques of weaving, plaiting, twining, and coiling. The instructions for each individual project will give you all the information necessary for completing that project, including the tools and materials you will need.

For inspiration, the gallery section features the work of 26 prominent basket makers. On page 115, there is a feature article on the work of Rob Dobson, who shares his work and artistic vision with you for creating baskets from alternative materials.

Once you've completed a few projects, it is my hope that you will feel confident enough to experiment on your own. As you will find, the exploration of the form is endless and the materials unlimited. Try matching unlikely materials with traditional techniques, or modify traditional techniques to the materials you use.

Making baskets from new materials is a wonderful marriage of vision and ingenuity. Once you start, you are embarking on a creative path of no return. No matter what material comes to mind, you will be thinking how you can weave it, plait it, twine it, or coil it into a basket. Above all, play and have fun!

MATERIALS

While it's easy to find suppliers of traditional basket-making materials, you are left to your own devices when making baskets from new materials. You may even find yourself in some unlikely places. Just think of it as a big treasure hunt!

Most often the materials will inspire ideas for your design. If you don't know where to begin, start browsing in hardware, craft- and art-supply, or fabric stores. Taking time to look at potential materials will generate an abundance of ideas, and you will start to visualize an incredible array of baskets.

Allow me to offer a warning to the pack rats among you. Once you start this process, you will consider almost everything you see as potential material for a basket. If you do have a problem with accumulating, you may find yourself swamped with a variety of wire, hardware, paper, containers, cardboard, and plastics for that I'll-make-it-someday basket.

If you are a beginner, you may want to visit a supplier of traditional materials to familiarize yourself with comparable materials before you go seeking reasonable (or unreasonable!) substitutes. You may also want to try your hand at making a few baskets with traditional materials to get an understanding of the techniques involved. Then, when you do go out looking for alternative materials, you will know which techniques are more suitable for the materials you find. (See *Techniques* on page 9.)

Keep in mind that the majority of traditional materials are dried plant matter. In order to make them pliable again, you need to soak them before use, and must keep them moist as you work. You may not need to follow this procedure when working with alternative materials. Let the materials be your guide. For instance, some papers and cardboard may be more easily manipulated when damp.

Assortment of Alternative Materials clockwise from top: thread, wire, bark, papers, rope, cardboard, clothesline, copper findings, twine, raffia, screen, dried natural material, ribbon, beads, and strapping tape.

Where to Look:

Start at home. Before you go in quest of new materials, first look around your immediate surroundings. You may be surprised (or shocked!) at what you already have that can be made into a wonderfully creative basket. Scraps and leftovers from other projects will often provide just what you need. Recyclable materials, such as old cardboard boxes, plastic bottles, plastic bags, or even tin cans, may become the inspiration for a project.

Hardware stores will yield many ideas and more materials than you can use. You'll find a large variety of wire, chains, sheet metal, nails, screening, washers, and roping under one roof. You may also find precut pieces of wood to use for bases, and strips of wood veneer to weave.

Craft- or art-supply stores allow you to look at many frequently used materials in a very different way. Buckets of beads or buttons can be incorporated into a coiled design. Polymer clay will make a wonderful basket. Use handmade papers, paper pulp, or papier-mâché. Foil papers, raffia, waxed linen thread, yarn, sheets of copper to cut and weave—all inspire ideas.

Fabric stores, aside from fabrics, offer ribbons, interfacing, tape measures, bindings, webbing, and batting. The core for making bias cording is an excellent start for a coiled basket, or an interesting texture in a twined or woven basket. Plus you'll find fancy cording, braids, and tassels that can enhance a design.

Your garden is a great source of potential material. Generally, you will dry the plant matter after you gather it, then soak it before use to make it pliable again. Dried iris or day lily leaves make perfect weavers. Why not corn husks, dried flowers, or flower stems? Try grape vines, periwinkle, honeysuckle, and willow. Be careful to avoid damaging a perennial plant, vine, tree, or shrub by taking too much at one time. You can also go on an expedition for cattails or wild grasses. Always observe proper gathering etiquette by asking before taking.

Scrap and salvage yards may be places you don't usually visit, but they can be a rich source of interesting materials (i.e., some really neat stuff!). Depending on the yard's specialty, you can find discarded wire and cable, hardware of all descriptions, copper findings, car and machine parts, laminated papers, and plastic tubing. Best of all, the materials are usually priced by weight, so you pay much less than retail rates. The inventory changes daily. If you see something you might be able to use, don't wait to buy it; you may not be able to find it the next time you return.

TOOLS

The tools you use will be determined by the materials you have at hand. For instance, if you are working with wire or metal, wire cutters will be much more useful than scissors. Designers provide a specific tool list for each project. However, there are tools common to traditional basket making that will help you as you create your projects. They are few and simple, and you may already have some of them in your family tool chest.

Awls, with their thin pointed ends, are handy

for making room in tight spaces when inserting the ends of a weaver. You can also use an awl to make holes for lashing materials together or for creating decorative effects.

Clamps or clothespins will give you an extra pair of hands for holding materials together when you begin certain weaving techniques, or for help in shaping materials as you weave. Many basket makers prefer the humble and inexpensive clothespin (only use the ones with springs), since its lighter grip is gentle to more delicate materials. If you are working on miniature baskets or in very tight spaces, use *mini or micro-mini alligator clips*. These small clamps, which you can find in electronics stores, have been known to save the sanity of many basketmakers.

Cutters, both for wire and for thicker materials, are essential. Small *wire cutters*, sometimes called *diagonal cutting pliers*, will cut the thinner gauges of wire (up to 14 gauge). For thicker wire, sheet metal, vines, or rope, you will need sturdy spring-loaded *tin snips* or *pruning shears*. Never use pruning shears on metal. Some designers recommend using a *pasta machine* for cutting paper into uniform strips. You may want to consider keeping a separate pasta machine just for craft purposes (a pasta machine is also a handy tool when working with polymer clay) to avoid contaminating your food. You will also need a good pair of *scissors*.

A pocket knife may be all that you will need for most of your cutting or carving needs in a project. Depending on the materials you are using, you may find that a *craft knife* or a *utility knife* works best.

Needle-nose pliers, with their long thin jaws, go where other pliers can't. While you will most often

Basic Tools clockwise from top: awl, diagonal wire cutters, micro-mini alligator clips, needle-nose pliers, tin snips, mini alligator clips, clamps, craft knife, scissors, L-square, tapestry needles, craft glue, and clothespins.

use them to grab materials to bring them through narrow spaces, you may also find yourself using them as a needle to guide lashing materials. Needle-nose pliers with smooth jaws may be more desirable when working with metal or wire, since the jaws will not mar the metal. However, pliers with serrated jaws are better when you need to grab and pull materials.

Measures, whether a *tape measure*, *ruler*, or *T-square*, ensure accuracy. Some traditional basket techniques rely on measuring by eye, and many basketmakers develop a good eye for this over time. If you're not that skilled yet, always use a measure for best results. Consider purchasing a long metal ruler or yardstick to use as a straightedge when cutting strips of material.

Other items you may need, depending on the project, will be pencils for marking, hot glue, white craft glue, masking tape, darning or tapestry needles, assorted paints, and general craft supplies. Some projects include materials that require soaking in water before use to make them pliable. Make sure you have a bucket, tub, or sink available for this purpose. Once you remove the soaked material, wrap it in an old towel to prevent it from drying out as you work. Also, use a spray bottle filled with water to moisten the materials as needed.

TECHNIQUES

Different basket-making techniques are more suitable than others when working with certain materials. Knowing the traditional techniques will help you decide which technique to use with the new materials you choose.

The variety of basket-making techniques evolved from the plant materials that were readily available within different geographic locations. An area with an abundance of soft grasses allowed the development of plaiting techniques that rely on weaving together materials that are similar in shape, size, and flexibility. An area with deciduous trees and viny shrubs allowed the development of weaving and twining techniques that rely on manipulating flexible weavers around rigid stakes or spokes.

If you aren't already familiar with them, get to know the traditional materials through a trip to a supplier, time with a catalog, or visit to a website. By understanding the basic properties of the materials (whether they are flat, round, extremely flexible, or rigid) you'll better understand what they can do within a technique. When it comes time to select new materials, you will be better able to compare and substitute.

For every traditional material, you will be able to find an alternative material that is similar to it in basic qualities. For instance, paper and plastic sheeting are good substitutes for rush, while wire and thin plastic tubing are good substitutes for round reed. Therefore, the paper and plastic will be more suitable for techniques traditionally associated with rush, as the wire and tubing will be for techniques traditionally associated with round reed.

When you are ready to match materials with a technique, begin by asking yourself a few questions. Is the material rigid enough to act as stake, spoke, or rib, or is it more suitable for use as a weaver? Does the material have enough body (its degree of internal strength) for the technique, or too much body, which will make it difficult to manipulate? Do I want a flat or more textured surface? If needed, can I easily cut this material to make weavers of equal width? If I coil this material, will it easily adapt to the shape I'm seeking?

Of course, keep in mind that there are no rules when pairing materials with techniques when making baskets from new materials. Sometimes the juxtaposition of a material's characteristic with an uncharacteristic technique creates a most wonderful basket. You may also figure out some extraordinary methods of engineering materials into a basket that have nothing to do with traditional techniques whatsoever. The best rule of thumb to follow is: Know your techniques (whatever they are) and materials; if you can make them work together, you will be able to produce a basket.

The basic information presented in the following sections is intended as a brief overview to get you started with the projects. They will provide you with a general knowledge of the different basket-making techniques used in this book.

Each technique has many variations—I'm convinced they're infinite. Beyond the basics found here, the designers have provided any additional, specific information as needed within their individual project instructions.

When finished, the base will be the approximate measurement you've determined for the length and width or diameter of your basket, as shown in figure 9.

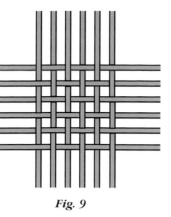

Fig. 9

Once you've woven the elements, you will need to *true* the base. To do this, begin by evening the ends of the stakes. Then adjust the stakes so the distance between them is the measurement you want for your design. As you work, you will need to go back and forth between the horizontal and vertical stakes to ease them into the correct position. Adjust the corners of the square or rectangle, making sure they are at right angles to each other. Depending on the material, use a pencil or marking pen to mark the corners of the square or rectangle on both the horizontal and vertical stakes, as shown in figure 10; then if the material shifts, you can

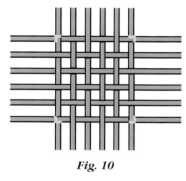

Fig. 10

easily realign the corners. You may find it helpful to place push pins just outside the corners as a guide for keeping them squared. You can also place clothespins or clamps on the corners to hold them at right angles.

TURNING UP THE STAKES

Now you are ready to turn up the sides. While the stakes are referred to as the rigid elements within a woven basket, the degree of rigidity varies according to the materials you use. When you turn the stakes up, they may or may not stand upright by themselves. If they don't, the first few rows of weaving will shape the basket and help direct the stakes upward.

For a Square or Rectangular Basket

For a square or rectangular basket, lay a ruler along the edge of your base. Bend the stakes at right angles to the straight edge of the ruler as shown in

figure 11. You may find it helpful to score some materials before bending them, such as stiff paper, thick felt, or cardboard. To get sharp, squared corners that define a rectangle or square, take care when turning up the corner stakes. Make sure to keep the corners square while you bend sharp, straight creases in the stakes.

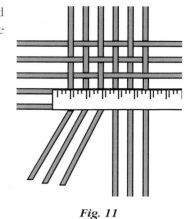

Fig. 11

For a Round or Oval Basket

Making a round or oval basket from a square or rectangular base is commonly know as working a square base to round. While the base is made exactly the same as for a square or rectangular basket, you will need to turn up the corner stakes in a different way to create the rounded shape.

After truing the base, you may find it helpful to use a pencil or marker to lightly sketch rounded corners around the woven square corners, as shown in figure 12. Then bend the corner stakes as shown in figure 13. It's important that the rounded corner stakes stay side by side. Use clamps if needed to keep them close together.

As you weave the first few rows, pull the weaver a bit tighter as you round the corners. This extra tension will round the corners to give you the shape you seek. Be careful though, you do not want to pull the weaver too tightly—this can draw the stakes inward and ultimately distort the shape of the basket.

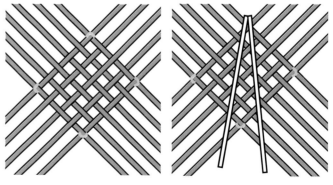

Fig. 12   **Fig. 13**

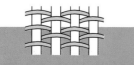

Weaving the Sides

Weaving the first few rows is the most awkward step in making a basket, and one of the most crucial. If the stakes do not stand upright by themselves, they will tend to flop in all directions. Clothespins and clamps can help to keep them under control.

Keep in mind that an even or odd number of stakes will affect your weaving pattern. With an even number of stakes, you will be weaving individual rows and will need to start and stop a weaver with each round. This method works well when weaving flat materials, and is particularly suited to weaving new materials that are both wide and flat with limited flexibility.

Start your weaver on the outside of the basket, weave around, then continue weaving beyond the starting point by four stakes before cutting the end of the weaver. To avoid a bulge from continuously starting and stopping in the same place, turn the basket a quarter turn before starting each new weaver.

With an uneven number of stakes, you can work a continuous weave. Because you are not starting and stopping, the weaving goes much faster. Continuous weave makes a spiral effect around the basket, which you can use to your advantage for creating decorative effects. Flat materials that are not too wide, and round materials work well as weavers for continuous weave. If you have an even number of stakes or spokes and want to make an uneven number, split one of the stakes in half to the base of a basket with a woven base, and to the center of the base of a round basket.

You can also alter your weaving pattern by carrying the weaver over and under the stakes or spokes in different ways, rather than the standard over one, under one. If you are in the mood to experiment, twill weaves (see page 10) will provide you with endless pattern variations.

As you weave, be mindful of keeping an even tension; if the tension is too tight, the sides will draw in, and if it is too loose, the sides will flare out. You can intentionally use varying degrees of tension to shape your basket—this can lead to some interesting effects and is worth exploring. When you have finished weaving, trim the ends of the stakes or spokes to make them even.

Making a Rim and Adding Handles

The design of your basket, your personal preference, and the materials you use will determine how you finish a woven basket. The easiest and most standard method of finishing a woven basket is to add on a separate edging known as a rim. (Be aware that the last row of weaving is called the *false rim*.) You can tuck the ends into the basket; however, this is a method associated more with plaiting techniques and will be discussed in that section on page 42.

The most common rim, as shown in figure 14, is made with two strips of material, each cut slightly longer than the measurement around the top of the finished basket. The strips, one placed on the outside edge of the basket with ends overlapped, and one on the inside, are lashed onto the edge with a thinner, more pliable material. If desired, you can place another length of rounded material at the very top of the stakes, laying it in the gap between the inside and outside strips.

Place clothespins or clamps around the edge of the basket to keep the strips in place as you work. The lashing is usually made with a simple overhand stitch (also called a whip or blanket stitch) that progresses around the basket by passing the stitch through the spaces between the stakes or spokes. You can also attach the rim to the edge using nails or rivets. If you are working with paper or cardboard, you can glue the strips on the edge.

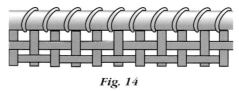

Fig. 14

The design of your basket determines when you will attach the handles. Some projects attach the handles after the weaving is complete and before attaching the rims. You can also secure the handle in the rim before lashing the rim by placing the ends of the handle between the basket and one of the rim components.

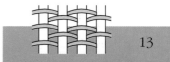

Colorful Cubes

Create these quick and easy cubes as a way to experiment with two-color design. When you're finished, you will have practical and colorful storage for a shelf or desk top. Or, use them as unique baskets for serving snacks at a casual party or picnic.

Designer: JOANNE WOOD PETERS

MATERIALS

Poster paper in one or two colors
Cardboard box with a 6-inch-square (15 cm) base
White craft glue
Waxed linen thread or fine string

TOOLS

Scissors
Small alligator clips, found in electronics stores
String
Tapestry needle
Paper cutter or manual pasta machine (optional)

INSTRUCTIONS

Finished dimensions: 6 inches (15 cm) square

1 Using the scissors (or paper cutter or pasta machine), cut the papers lengthwise into strips that are ½ inch (1.3 cm) wide. These will be used as the stakes and weavers. Use some of the paper for cutting additional lengthwise strips that are ¼ inch (.6 cm) wide. You can use these thinner strips as weavers to vary the design of the basket, as shown in the bottom basket in the photo.

2 Weave the base. Use 18 strips, nine horizontal and nine vertical. If you are working with two colors, alternate the colors. Weave the strips over one, under one. True the base, and use small clips to hold the corners in place.

3 Since the paper is very flexible, it is easier to weave the basket if you use a form. I used a 6-inch-square (15 cm) cardboard box. Place the box on the woven base, and turn the stakes upright. To keep the stakes in place until you weave the first few rows, tie a string around the box and upright stakes.

4 Weave the sides. All rows are start-stop, using an over one, under one weave. To begin, take one weaver and place it on top of or under (see Tip below) one stake, using a small alligator clip to secure it. Weave around the basket. As you weave around each corner, use an alligator clip at each corner to help square them.

5 At the end of the row, overlap the end of the weaver by four stakes, ending the weaver behind a stake. Put a dab of glue on the end of the weaver to secure it to the stake. Use a small clip to hold the end in place until the glue is dry. Turn the basket one-quarter turn to the left and start weaving the next row. When you get to a corner, remove the clip from the previous row and clip the corner of the new row. Continue for 11 rows.

6 To finish, trim the width of a ½-inch (1.3 cm) weaver by approximately ⅛ inch (.3 cm). Weave one more row using this trimmed weaver (this last row is called a false rim). Remove the basket from the form.

7 Fold the stakes that are on the inner side of the false rim over the false rim to the outside, then trim the ends of the stakes to be slightly shorter than the false rim. Glue the ends, holding them with small clips until the glue dries. Fold the outer stakes to the inside; trim, glue, and clip.

8 To make the rim, take two ½-inch-wide (1.3 cm) strips, placing one around the inside and one around the outside of the false rim to cover the folded stakes. Overlap the ends. Use clips to hold the strips in place. Using the needle and thread, use an overhand stitch to lash the rim by passing the needle and thread between each stake. Work around the rim, then secure the thread with a few overhand stitches, and knot. Work the thread back through the rim, burying it between the elements before cutting it off.

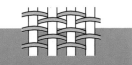

TIP: Note the middle and top baskets in the photo. This is a good example of how a simple variation can change the look of your basket. The first row of the middle basket is made with a white weaver that is first woven over one blue stake, than under one white stake. The top basket begins with a white weaver that is first woven over one white stake, then under one blue stake.

Speaker Wire Cat's Head Basket

Technology touches tradition with this cat's head basket made from speaker wire. The cat's-head-shaped bottom, devised by the Shakers, is a practical way to make a round basket from a square base. You form the cat's head while weaving the first few rows of the sides. You'll find that the wire easily retains the shape as you work.*

Designer: **JOANNE WOOD PETERS**

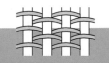

MATERIALS

30-foot (9 m) spool of 24-gauge speaker wire, clear
plastic-coated with copper wire showing through
75-foot (23 m) spool of 18-gauge speaker wire,
clear plastic-coated with copper wire
showing through
Narrow strip of metal (can be cut from a can), or a
strip of plastic of medium rigidity

TOOLS

Wire cutters
Scissors
Clothespins

INSTRUCTIONS

Finished dimensions: Base, 3½ x 3½ inches (8.8 x
8.8 cm); height, 3 inches (7.5 cm); rim diameter, 6
inches (15 cm)

1 Cut the 24-gauge wire, which will be used for
the stakes, into 18 equal pieces, each approximately 18 to 20 inches (45 to 50 cm) long.

2 Using the 24-gauge wire, weave an open-weave
base, over one, under one. To make the open
weave, leave some space between the wires as you
weave. You will have nine stakes (pieces of wire)
woven horizontally, and nine woven vertically. True
the base, making sure there is an equal amount of
space between the wires.

3 Use the 18-gauge wire to weave the sides in an
over one, under one weave. You will be working a continuous weave over an even number of
stakes to give the basket its diagonal pattern. To do
this, you will need to adjust the weave as you work
around the basket. Begin weaving the first row. When
you reach the point where the weave will repeat,
weave behind two stakes. This will create a diagonal
pattern on the inside of the basket. If you want a diagonal pattern on the outside of the basket, weave over
two stakes on the outside of the basket when you
reach the point where the weave will repeat.

4 You will create the cat's head for the base while
weaving the first few rows. To do this, weave
one side, then use your fingers to pull the corners of
the base down, while pushing the bottom of the base
up with your thumbs. You want to make a nice slop-
ing curve between the corners of the base. Repeat this

after weaving each side of each row. Once you finish
the first 12 rows of weaving, the cat's head shape
should be well defined.

5 If you need to start a new weaver, overlap the
ends of the old and new weavers by approximately four stakes, and continue weaving as before.
Weave approximately 23 rows, making sure to reserve
enough wire for lashing the rim of the basket. Do not
cut the ends of the stakes.

6 To make the rim, cut a piece from the metal or
plastic that measures ¼ inch (.6 cm) wide and 4
inches (10 cm) longer than the rim circumference. For
the lasher, cut a length of 18-gauge wire that is
approximately twice the circumference of the rim.
Place the metal strip on the outside of the basket in
front of the stakes, and down against the top row of
weaving. Use clothespins to secure the strip to the
basket.

7 You will be creating a scalloped edge by bending the stakes behind the lashed rim. To do this,
begin by threading the lasher between two stakes,
placing it between the top row of weaving and the
rim. You want the end of the lasher to be on the outside of the basket. Now, bring the long end of the
lasher straight up and over the rim (from the inside of
the basket to the outside), bringing it down, across,
and under the rim, then threading it between the same
stakes.

8 On the inside of the basket, cross the lasher in
back of the rim, placing it diagonally to the right
and under the rim. Bring the lasher up over the rim in
the same space. At the same time, take the stake to
the left, and bend it diagonally to the right. Bring the
lasher over the stake and under the rim in the next
space to the right, and again take the next stake to the
left and bend it diagonally to the right. Continue in
this way around the basket. To end the lashing, repeat
a few extra overlaps at the beginning of the rim row
before cutting the end of the lasher.

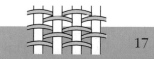

Copper and Aluminum Cat's Head Basket

Metal strips of copper and aluminum, used for the weavers, create a basket that is unique, handsome, and functional. Wire mesh provides a framework for weaving the basket's speaker-wire stakes. Making the cat's head base is easy since the metal mesh holds the shape.

Designer: **JOANNE WOOD PETERS**

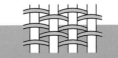

MATERIALS

One 24-inch-square (61 cm) piece of ¼-inch
(.6 cm) wire mesh

18-gauge speaker wire, clear plastic-coated with
copper wire showing through

⅛-inch (.3 cm) and ¼-inch (.6 cm) copper foil,
available where stained glass supplies are sold

¼-, ⅜-, and ½-inch (.6 cm, .9 cm, 1.3 cm),
aluminum foil, used for house siding, available
at hardware and home-supply stores

Long, narrow copper beads (approximately the
width of the speaker wire) with lengthwise holes

Gray waxed linen thread or clear fishing line

TOOLS

Wire cutters
Scissors
Tapestry needle

INSTRUCTIONS

Finished dimensions: Base, 4 x 4 inches
(10 x 10 cm); height, 4 inches (10 cm); rim
diameter, 8 inches (20 cm)

1 In the middle of the piece of mesh, plot a 4½-
inch (11.3 cm) square. To do this, count the
smaller squares of the mesh so you have 18 vertically
and 18 horizontally. You want the square to be cen-
tered with an even amount of mesh on each side. You

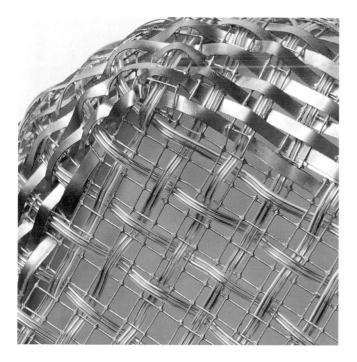

may find it helpful to mark the outer edges of the
square. Using the wire cutters, cut from the outer edge
of the piece of mesh to the corners of the 4½-inch
(11.3 cm) square, making two cuts top to bottom and
two cuts bottom to top.

2 With the wire cutters, cut out the connecting
horizontal wires between every other vertical
column in the mesh, giving you nine stakes on each
side of the square. Weave the speaker wire, vertically
and horizontally, through every other hole in the
mesh. Turn these stakes upright.

3 Using a start-stop weave, you will weave the
sides following this pattern:

12 rows of ⅛-inch (.3 cm) copper strips
3 rows of ¼-inch (.6 cm) aluminum
3 rows of ¼-inch (.6 cm) copper
1 row of ¼-inch (.6 cm) aluminum
2 rows of ¼-inch (.6 cm) copper
1 row of ⅜-inch (.9 cm) aluminum

4 You will create the cat's head for the base while
weaving the first few rows. To do this, weave
one side (using the ⅛-inch [.3 cm] copper strips), then
use your fingers to pull the corners of the base down,
while pushing the bottom of the base up with your
thumbs. Repeat this after weaving each side of each
row. Once you finish the first 12 rows of weaving, the
cat's head shape should be well defined.

5 To make the rim, first string enough beads to fit
around the rim on a length of waxed linen
thread, then set aside. Cut two lengths of ½-inch
(1.3 cm) aluminum to go around the rim, allowing
enough extra length for overlapping the ends. Place
the two lengths of aluminum around the inside and
outside rim of the basket. Lay the string of copper
beads on top of the last row of weaving and between
the two lengths of aluminum. Use clips or clamps to
hold the strips in place.

6 Using fishing line or waxed linen thread, work
to the right to lash the rim by lacing through
each stake. When you return to your starting point,
reverse directions, and lash to the left. You want the
thread to cross over the top of the rim to secure the
beads. Secure the thread with a few overhand stitches
and a knot. Then work the thread back through the
rim, burying it between the elements before cutting.

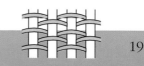

Laminated Paper with Curls

This basket has a double wall. To make it, you will weave two baskets,

Designer: JOANNE WOOD PETERS

one inside the other. Though it may sound complicated, it's really very easy. By weaving a double wall (sometimes called a double weave), you can create different effects for the inside and the outside of your baskets.

MATERIALS

Laminated marbleized paper in two colors
Cardboard box with a 7-inch-square (17.5 cm) base
Clear gimp (plastic lacing) found in craft stores

TOOLS

Scissors
Small alligator clips, found in electronics stores
String
Glue suitable for use on plastic
Needle
Paper cutter or manual pasta machine (optional)

INSTRUCTIONS

Finished dimensions: Base, 7 x 7 inches (17.5 cm); height, 11 inches (27.5 cm).

1 Using the scissors (or paper cutter or pasta machine), cut the laminated papers lengthwise into strips that are ½ inch (1.3 cm) wide. Use some of the paper for cutting into additional lengthwise strips that are ¼ inch (.6 cm) wide. These thinner strips, along with the ½-inch (1.3 cm) strips, will be used for the weavers. (I used a pasta machine to cut the ¼-inch (.6 cm) strips.)

2 Since the basket will have a double wall, you will use twice the amount of strips for your stakes. This basket takes 26 strips of each color, for a total of 52 strips. Arrange the strips in pairs consisting of one strip of each color. Place them back to back. Turn the strips with the color you want for the inside facing up, and the color you want for the outside facing down.

3 Keeping the paired strips with the inside color facing up, use a 2 x 2 twill (page 10) to weave the 26 strips, each pair woven as one strip, with 13 strips woven horizontally, and 13 woven vertically. Remember that a 2 x 2 twill is woven with two over and two under. True the base, adjusting the spaces between the stakes so the base measures 7 x 7 inches (17.5 x 17.5 cm). Use small clips to hold the corners of the square in place.

4 Since paper is very flexible, it is easier to weave the basket if you use a form. I used a 7-inch-square (17.5 cm) cardboard box. Place the box on the woven base. You'll notice an inside set of stakes and an outside set of stakes. You will weave the inner basket first. Turn the inside stakes upright and tie with a string to keep them in place until you weave the first few rows.

5 Begin weaving the sides of the inner basket. All rows are start-stop weave in an over one, under one weave. You want virtually no space between the stakes, so make the weave as tight as possible, without distorting the shape. Weave the inner basket following this pattern:
3 rows using ½-inch (1.3 cm) strips
7 rows using ¼-inch (.6 cm) strips
2 rows using ½-inch (1.3 cm) strips
5 rows using ¼-inch (.6 cm) strips
2 rows using ½-inch (1.3 cm) strips
7 rows using ¼-inch (.6 cm) strips
2 rows using ½-inch (1.3 cm) strips
When you've finished weaving the inner basket, place clips around the rim to keep it together while weaving the outer basket.

6 Begin weaving the outer basket. Turn the stakes for the outer basket upright over the form, and tie with a string to keep them in place until you weave the first few rows. For your weavers, use strips that are the same color as the stakes for the outer basket. As you weave, keep the stakes of the inner basket and outer basket in line with each other.

7 Begin with five rows of over one, under one start-stop weave, using ½-inch (1.3 cm) strips. The next several rows are woven in a chase weave (two weavers woven at once over an even number of stakes, one weaver starts and the other chases it around the basket). To begin the chase, take the clear gimp and place one end behind a stake, then weave around the basket. Using the scissors, taper the end of a ¼-inch (.6 cm) weaver approximately 5 inches (12.5 cm) in from the end. At the point where the gimp will start repeating the weave (after one row), insert the tapered end of the ¼-inch (.6 cm) weaver in front of the stake, just to the left of the stake where you started the gimp. Weave one round with the paper, then one with gimp. Since this is a continuous weave, you may need to add new weavers. If you do, simply glue the new weavers to the ends of the old. Repeat the chase weave until you have 16 rows using the ¼-inch (.6 cm) paper strips. End the row above the original taper, tapering the remaining end of the paper as above, then weave one more row of gimp. Finally, weave two rows using ½-inch (1.3 cm) strips.

8 To make the rim, trim the width of a ½-inch (1.3 cm) weaver by approximately ⅛ inch (.3 cm). Weave one more row using this trimmed weaver (this last row is called a false rim). When weaving the false rim you will treat the stakes for the inner and outer baskets as one, pairing them as you did for weaving the base. Remove the basket from the form.

9 Fit the inner rim using a ½-inch (1.3 cm) strip of the inner color, and the outer rim using a ½-inch (1.3 cm) strip of the outer color. Using small clips, clip them onto the false rim. Lash the rim with the clear gimp, using an overhand stitch, and passing the gimp between each stake.

10 To make the curls, use ¼-inch (.6 cm) strips of each color, pairing them back to back. Starting at one corner, insert the ends of one pair behind the top row that has been woven with a ¼-inch (.6 cm) paper, placing the ends to the right of the stake. Next, insert the other ends two rows down and to the left of the stake. Use your fingers or a tool handle to pull the strips to create the loops; using a tool handle will help to keep the loops a uniform size. Repeat this process, continuing all the way down the basket until you reach the first row of ½-inch (1.3 cm) strips. Glue the ends behind the stakes. Note: As shown in the photo, the rows of loops for this basket were worked diagonally to the right and left of the column, and up toward the opposite corners. The other side was done in the same way, except the opposite color was exposed.

11 To make the top curls, use ½-inch (1.3 cm) strips. Each curl is made separately. Insert one end behind the top row to the right of the stake and the other end to the left, one row down. Glue the ends.

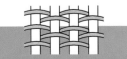

Polymer Clay Basket with Telephone Wire Embellishments

Making a basket with polymer clay provides you with a broad range of color choices. This one is dusted with metallic powders to give it an extra sheen. You will need to weave and bake the basket over a form. Once it's ready, you will have a strong and unique basket that is sure to get many compliments.

Designer: **SHEILA A. SHEPPARD**

MATERIALS

15 ounce (425 g) metal can, cleaned and empty

Aluminum foil

2 ounces (56 g) polymer clay: 1 ounce (28 g) black,
   1 ounce (28 g) dark purple,
   or colors of your choice

Metallic powders, used here: lilac,
   antique gold, and copper

Parchment paper

Multicolored telephone wire

TOOLS

Pasta machine

Ruler

Craft knife with fine blade

Bamboo skewer or piercing tool

Oven, conventional or convection

Oven timer

Oven thermometer

Baking sheet (glass or metal)

Wire cutters

Ruler

Dusting brush (for powders)

INSTRUCTIONS

1 Use a can with only one end open. Remove any paper labels. Wash and dry thoroughly. Invert the can, open end down, and cover the can loosely with three layered sheets of aluminum foil. Form the aluminum foil sheets to the shape of the can, but do not pack or press the layers too tightly; you want them to have a slight give. Set aside.

2 Mix 1 ounce (28 g) of the black polymer clay with 1 ounce (28 g) of the dark purple. Set the pasta machine on the thickest setting (usually #1). Run the clays through until well blended. Roll this mixture into a ball, then into an oval shape. Hand flatten the oval to a pancake approximately ¼ inch (.6 cm) thick.

3 Keeping the pasta machine on the thickest setting, run the narrow end of the clay pancake through the rollers; you want to end with a piece of clay that is 10 inches (25 cm) long and 3 inches (7.5 cm) wide. Lay this sheet of clay on a clean work surface. Using the craft knife and the ruler as a straightedge, cut the clay into eight pieces that are each ¼ inch (.6 cm) wide by 10 inches (25 cm) long.

4 Position the inverted, aluminum-covered can on your work space and evenly drape the eight strips of clay over the bottom end of the can to look like the spokes of a wheel. Check the spokes as they drape down the can, and adjust so the spacing between them is even. Prepare a thin, flat disk of polymer clay approximately 1¼ inches (3 cm) in diameter. Position it evenly over the clay spokes on the bottom of the can, like the hub of a wheel, and press it into the spokes.

5 Cut several ¼-inch-wide (.6 cm) strips from the flattened clay mixture. If needed, make more as in step 3. Starting at any point out from the hub, begin to weave the strips in an over one, under one pattern. To start the weaver, just press the end of it next to the hub. Continue to weave as you slowly spiral down and around the side of the can. As you weave, check that you have even spacing between rows. Add new weavers as needed, pressing the end of the old weaver to the end of the new weaver.

6 To make the rim, cut a band of clay approximately ¾ to 1 inch (1.9 to 2.5 cm) wide. Use this band to cover the ends of the spokes, attaching the band around the rim approximately 3½ inches (8.8 cm) down from the bottom of the can (which of course will be the top of the basket). Be sure to press the clay together lightly where the weave intersects. Flare the band out slightly.

7 Gently turn the can over. Using the bamboo skewer, make ¼-inch (.6 cm) holes that are opposite each other in the top band that is now the flared rim of the basket. Using a soft brush, dust the surface of the basket with metallic powders, blending the colors together as you brush. Be sure to dust the inside of the rim. (Applying the powders is optional.)

8 Place the thermometer in the oven, then set the oven temperature at 275ºF (135ºC). Line a baking dish with parchment paper. Place the basket, bottom side down with the can still inside, in the baking dish. Monitor the oven temperature. If it is not at 275ºF (135ºC), adjust the temperature before putting the basket in the oven. Set the timer for 40 minutes, and bake the basket.

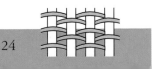

9 While the basket is baking, prepare the colored telephone wire. Combine enough colored wire in a group so the ends will fit easily through the ¼-inch (.6 cm) holes in the rim. With wire cutters, cut the grouped wire into two lengths, each 12 inches (30 cm) long. Group six pieces of wire and cut into two 6-inch (15 cm) lengths. Set the wire aside.

10 When the basket is finished baking, remove it from the oven and allow it to air cool until completely cool. Then slowly remove the can from the basket.

11 To create the basket handle, group the ends of one of the 12-inch (30 cm) lengths made in step 9. From the inside of the rim, push the ends gently through one of the ¼-inch (.6 cm) holes in the rim. Feed the wire to the outside of the rim until you have a 2-inch (5 cm) length, then bring the ends straight up. Gather one of the 6-inch (15 cm) lengths. Center it crosswise on the ends that are straight up, then wrap it around the 12 inch (30 cm) length, including the ends that are straight up, two times. Fray the ends of the 6-inch (15 cm) length by separating the ends. Then bend the end of the 12-inch (30 cm)

length down toward the rim. Repeat on the other side of the rim. Finally, take the second group of wires and gently weave them into the body of the basket, as shown in the photo.

Bird Feeder

Make this bird-feeder basket to hang in your garden. Use different vines for your weavers to add interest to the sides. Add feathers or other decorative ornamentation. Do a good deed by weaving in a little yarn, strips of fabric, or bits of cotton to provide the birds with easy-to-find nest material.

Designer: KAREN KAUSHANSKY

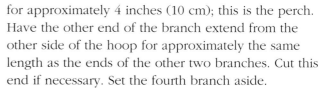

MATERIALS

60 inches (1.5 m) of willow or strong flexible vine, approximately ⅜ inch (.9 cm) in diameter

Four branches of willow, each approximately 50 inches (1.3 m) long

Thin vines for weavers such as ivy, blackberry, and thin willow

Wire or string

TOOLS

Pruning shears

Scissors

Long-nose pliers

INSTRUCTIONS

1 Make a hoop from the 60-inch (1.5 m) length of willow or any strong flexible vine. To do this, take the vine and circle it in the middle of its length, making a circle 6 to 8 inches (15 to 20 cm) in diameter. There will be two long ends extending from the circle. Weave these back and around the vine, encircling the hoop to secure its shape.

2 The four long branches will be your spokes. To secure them to the hoop, first place the hoop on your work surface. Taking two of the branches, lay one crosswise on the hoop, placing it approximately 1½ inches (3.8 cm) from the bottom of the circle. Take the other branch and place it parallel to the first branch, approximately 1½ inches (3.8 cm) from the top of the circle. Center these on the hoop so that the ends of the branches extending from the hoop are approximately equal in length.

3 Take the third branch and lay it perpendicular to the other branches, centering it on the hoop. Cut one end of the branch so it extends beyond the hoop for approximately 4 inches (10 cm); this is the perch. Have the other end of the branch extend from the other side of the hoop for approximately the same length as the ends of the other two branches. Cut this end if necessary. Set the fourth branch aside.

4 Beginning at one end of the hoop, use wild blackberry, ivy, or thin willow as the weavers that secure the branches to the hoop. Do an over and under weave, using the edges of the hoop and center (third) branch as spokes. Go back and forth from one side to the other until you are almost to the center. As you near the center of the hoop, add the fourth branch, placing it evenly across the hoop, threading it under the third branch. Continue weaving.

5 When the bottom is solidly woven, use a long-nose pliers to carefully bend the seven spokes upward. (Do not panic if a spoke breaks, simply work the broken end into the woven base at the same spot for approximately 2 inches [5 cm] and turn up again). Bring the spokes in at an angle until they meet (this will look like a tepee). Take a wire or string and wind it around this meeting point. You want the spokes to be fairly straight as they angle inward; you don't want any obvious bulges. Adjust the spokes as needed.

6 Again using a thin weaver, start at the top and weave in and out of the seven spokes, alternating over one, under one with each round. Continue this way around the feeder, adding weavers when needed, until you are approximately 4 inches (10 cm) from the base.

7 At this point, you will leave an opening on the side with the perch. Do this by weaving partially around the feeder rather than all the way around. Find

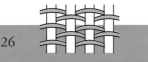

the two spokes that are on either side of the perch. When you get to one of these spokes, circle around it with the weaver, and weave back around the feeder. Then, when you get to the other spoke that is near the perch on the other side, circle around it, and weave back around the feeder. Continue in this way, weaving back and forth, until you reach the base.

8 At the base, plan on having a long end of a weaver. Weave the end around the hoop as well as along the spokes to secure it. Fill in any open spaces in the feeder with a back and forth weave. Using the wire or string, add a small loop at the top of the feeder, and it is ready to hang.

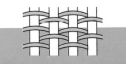

Twig and Moss Lampshade

Starting with a purchased metal frame, designer Dyan Peterson has created the perfect lampshade for a country cabin, or to remind a city dweller of that great vaca-tion in the mountains. Have fun looking for a rustic base to complete the lodge look.

Designer: **DYAN MAI PETERSON**

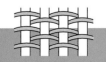

MATERIALS

Hexagonal metal lampshade frame; this one is a chimney top, but you can also use clip and finial styles as needed

Assortment of twigs with bark still on, look for twigs that are ¼ to ⅜ inch (.6 to .9 cm) in diameter

Raffia

Small pinecones, hemlock pinecones work well

Moss

Lichen

Translucent paper

Fire-retardant spray

TOOLS

Pruning shears

Hot glue gun and glue sticks

Scissors

INSTRUCTIONS

Finished dimensions: Base, 10½ by 12 inches (26 x 30 cm); height 6 inches (15 cm)

1 Gather the twigs. You want them to be between ¼ inch (.6 cm) and ⅜ inch (.9 cm) in diameter. Keep the bark on. The size of the frame, plus the thickness of the twigs, will determine the amount of twigs you will need. This number will vary. The best strategy is to know the dimensions of your frame, and have an ample amount of twigs on hand to cut as you need them.

2 The twigs are overlapped at their ends, log-cabin style. When cutting the twigs, keep in mind that their ends will overlap by approximately 1 to 1½ inches (2.5 to 3.8 cm) on each end. Therefore, factor in an additional 2 to 3 inches (5 to 7.5 cm) to the measurement of each twig before cutting them. Note also that the sides of this shade slope; the length of all twigs will be graduated to accommodate the slope.

3 Measure one side of the frame at its bottom. Add 2 to 3 inches (2.5 to 3.8 cm) to this measurement. Using the pruning shears, cut six twigs to this measurement. Weave one twig into one side of the frame; one end of the twig will be under the frame, one end will be over. Take another twig, lay it over the end of the first twig log-cabin style, and glue the overlap with hot glue. Move around the frame, weaving the ends into the frame, overlapping the ends, and gluing them together. Continue in this way, cutting twigs as needed, and work your way up the side of the shade. If your frame slopes, you will need to cut graduated lengths as the side moves upward.

4 Embellish the shade once all the twigs are in place. Cut six 6-inch (15 cm) lengths of raffia. Tie one around two twigs where they overlap at an angle on the hexagon. Repeat at the remaining five angles. (I only did this once around the shade, but you can tie more raffia lengths as desired.) Using the hot glue gun, attach the pinecones where desired. Weave the moss and lichen through the twigs, and glue in place.

5 When the outside of the shade is decorated, finish the inside. Measure the inside of the shade, and cut a lining from the translucent paper to fit. Using the hot glue gun, glue the lining to the shade. Glue only between the paper and the twigs, since you do not want the glue to be close to the bulb. Following the manufacturer's instructions, spray the lining of the shade with fire-retardant spray.

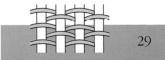

Woven Ribbon Basket

By using wired ribbon to weave over a form, you can create a stunning gift container that will be treasured long after the gift is forgotten. Best of all, with all the beautiful ribbons available today, the most trouble you'll have making this easy-to-weave basket is deciding which ribbons to use.

Designer: **Dyan Mai Peterson**

Materials

Papier-mâché lidded box, 4½ inches (11.3 cm) in diameter by 5½ inches (13.8 cm) tall, can be purchased in a craft supply store

Matte-finish spray paint in black or color of your choice

8 yards (7.5 m) of 1½-inch (3.8 cm) ribbon, 4½ yards (4 m) of color A, and 3½ yards (3 m) of color B (wired ribbon works best)

2 yards (1.8 m) of ¼-inch (.6 cm) ribbon, in black or color of your choice

Perle cotton #5, 1 skein in black or color of your choice

Waxed linen thread in black or color of your choice

Chinese coin

Assorted beads

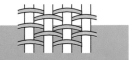

Tools

Scissors
Small alligator clips
Hot glue gun and glue sticks
Toothpicks
Needle

Instructions

1 Using the spray paint, spray the inside and outside of the container and lid. Allow to dry. You will get better results applying two light coats, allowing the first coat to dry thoroughly before applying the second.

2 Cut four 20-inch (50 cm) lengths of the 1½-inch (3.8 cm) ribbon in color A; these will be the spokes for the container. Cut four 10-inch (25 cm) lengths of the 1½-inch (3.8 cm) ribbon in color A; these will be the spokes for the lid. Using a pencil, lightly mark the center point of each spoke. For the weavers, cut three 16-inch (40 cm) lengths of the 1½-inch (3.8 cm) ribbon in color B, and four 16-inch (40 cm) lengths of the ¼-inch (.6 cm) ribbon.

3 Arrange the spokes for the container. Take one of the 20-inch (50 cm) lengths of ribbon and lay it vertically on your work surface. Take another 20-inch (50 cm) length and lay it horizontally over the vertical length, lining up their center points. Using a small drop of hot glue, glue them together at their centers. Take another length of ribbon and lay it crosswise over the two spokes. Again line up the center points, and apply the glue. Finally, take the remaining length and lay it crosswise in the other direction, line it up, then glue it. The ribbons will resemble the spokes of a wheel. Note: To get the right amount of glue and to avoid the trailing threads of hot glue, I use a toothpick or the end of a small awl as an applicator, taking a drop of the hot glue from the tip of the glue gun.

4 Place the container upright on the spokes, positioning it over the center of the spokes. Bring one of the spokes up the side of the container. Fold the end of the spoke over the container's top edge to the inside of the container. Use a micro-mini alligator clip to hold the ribbon to the container. Do the same with all remaining spokes.

5 Weave the sides using a start-stop weave in an over one, under one pattern. Alternate the thin ribbon with the wide ribbon, weaving the first row with the ¼-inch (.6 cm) ribbon. Weave each row, then go back and glue the ends of the weaver underneath the spoke (using only the smallest amount of glue) before weaving the next row. The last row will be woven with the thin ribbon.

6 Remove a clip from one of the spokes. Fold the ribbon in on itself until the length of the spoke is even with the top of the container. Trim the fold, leaving a ½-inch (1.3 cm) allowance. Glue the fold to the container, again using a small amount of glue. Repeat for all the spokes.

7 For the rim, open the skein of perle cotton. Without removing any individual strands, divide the skein in half, making a large circle. Cut the skein at one point on the circle. Wrap the skein around the rim of the container, arranging it as you please. Leave approximately 8 inches (20 cm) free for tying the ends and making the tassel. Glue the skein in place around the rim of the basket, slipping the Chinese coin onto one end. Tie the ends into a decorative knot. At the base of the knot, use an end of the cotton to wrap the top of the tassel, securing the end with an overhand knot.

8 For the lid, arrange the spokes as you did for the bottom of the container; do not glue them. Lay the lid, top down, on the spokes. Bring the ends of the spokes over the edge of the lid, holding them in place with alligator clips. Fold each of the ends of the spokes over on themselves to hide any raw edges, then glue the ends to the inside edge of the lid.

9 To finish, string beads on the waxed linen thread and attach them close to the knot at the rim of the container. Make a small decorative bow from any remaining ribbon in color B. Using an 8-inch (20 cm) length of ¼-inch (.6 cm) ribbon, attach the bow at its middle to the center point of the top spoke. If desired, embellish the ends of the thin ribbon with small beads.

31

Bamboo and Paper Lantern

Weave this basket without a bottom to create a lantern for a tall votive candle. While the bamboo suggests a tropical setting, use the lantern wherever you live to light up a porch gathering on a balmy summer night. Alter the design to make lanterns in different sizes for a dramatic grouping.

Designer: **DYAN MAI PETERSON**

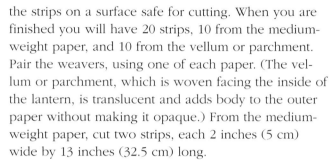

MATERIALS

½-inch (1.3 cm) foam core
1 large sheet of medium-weight, translucent paper
1 large sheet of vellum or parchment paper
Bamboo, approximately ¼ inch (.6 cm) in diameter, enough to cut twelve, 14-inch (35 cm) lengths
Waxed linen thread
Chinese coins, approximately 24, can be purchased in a bead shop
Thin sticks, cut into pieces approximately 1 to 1½ inches (2.5 to 3.8 cm) long (the length of the piece should be slightly longer than the diameter of the coin), one piece per coin
Assorted beads

TOOLS

Pencil
Craft knife
Long ruler/straightedge
Hot glue gun and glue sticks
Needle

INSTRUCTIONS

Finished dimensions: Diameter, 25 inches (63.5 cm); height 14 inches (35 cm)

1 On the foam core, draw or trace a circle with a 24½-inch (62 cm) diameter. Use the craft knife to cut the circle out, and set aside. You will use this as a form to help the lantern keep its shape. Cut the bamboo to get 12 lengths, each 14 inches (35 cm) long; these will be the stakes.

2 Cut the weavers from the papers. On each sheet of paper, measure and mark the cutting lines to make 10 strips, each 1½ inches (3.8 cm) wide by 25 inches (63.5 cm) long. I find it's easier to cut the strips using a straightedge and craft knife. Make sure you cut the strips on a surface safe for cutting. When you are finished you will have 20 strips, 10 from the medium-weight paper, and 10 from the vellum or parchment. Pair the weavers, using one of each paper. (The vellum or parchment, which is woven facing the inside of the lantern, is translucent and adds body to the outer paper without making it opaque.) From the medium-weight paper, cut two strips, each 2 inches (5 cm) wide by 13 inches (32.5 cm) long.

3 Lay the bamboo lengths on a flat surface. Weave the strips in an over-under pattern with the medium-weight paper facing up, and the vellum or parchment side facing down. Make the bottom edge of the first row even with the bottom edge of the bamboo. Position the two end stakes 1½ inches (3.8 cm) in from the ends of the weavers. Adjust the distance between the stakes accordingly, making sure the spaces are even.

4 Determine where you will place the Chinese coins. You can place them randomly or in a pattern. Just make sure to distribute them evenly over the surface of the weaving to better secure the stakes. Thread a needle with waxed linen thread; don't knot the end. Sew through the paper and around a bamboo stake. Cut the thread to leave two ends, each approximately 3 inches (7.5 cm) long. Thread both ends through the hole in a Chinese coin. Take one length of thin stick, and place it on top of the coin. Using a double knot, tie the two ends of the thread around the stick. If desired, thread assorted beads on the ends, then knot them to secure the beads. Repeat for all coins.

5 Cover the ends of the weavers. Fold both 2-inch-wide (5 cm) strips in half lengthwise. Using hot

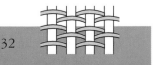

glue, glue a folded strip over the ends of the weavers on one side, then repeat with the other strip on the other side. Then overlap the bands and glue. Stand the lantern up. To help keep the lantern's shape, take the piece of foam core cut in step 1 and position the lantern around it. You may need to trim the foam-core circle to fit the inner measurement of the lantern.

6 **Caution:** Only use with a votive candle in a glass holder. Never place the lantern directly in contact with an open flame. If desired, you could treat the lantern with a flame-retardant spray.

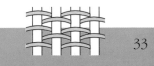

Handmade Paper Basket

Take advantage of the wonderful textured and colorful hand-made papers that are readily available today in art-supply stores. By soaking strips of paper, then weaving them over a form, you can make a range of appealing baskets in no time.

Designer: **DYAN MAI PETERSON**

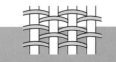

MATERIALS

Handmade paper, medium to heavyweight
Plastic wrap
Acrylic gloss medium in a matte or semi-gloss finish
Beads, charms, or other embellishments, as desired

TOOLS

Bowl with a smooth surface
Bucket, bowl, or sink for soaking the paper
Craft knife
Paintbrushs

INSTRUCTIONS

1 Enjoy selecting your handmade papers! Look for medium to heavyweight papers, avoiding those that may have large leaves or twigs embedded in the fibers.

2 Select a bowl to use as your form. Look for one with a smooth surface. Avoid bowls with cut-work, etching, raised glazes, or surface grooves or ridges. Invert the bowl, then wrap the outer surface with lengths of plastic wrap, tucking the wrap around the rim and into the bowl. Smooth the wrap, making it lay as flat as possible.

3 Using the formula base + height + height (see page 10) figured from the measurement of the bowl, determine how long your stakes will be. The size of your form and the design for your basket will also determine how many stakes you will need. Cut or rip the strips for your stakes from the paper. Ripping adds extra textural interest.

4 You will be weaving the basket using a start-stop weave in an over one, under one pattern. Cut or rip enough strips from the paper to accommodate this technique.

5 Soak the paper in warm water that completely covers the strips. Gently move the strips so all surfaces get wet. The length of time you need to soak the paper is different with individual papers. You want the strips to be soaked through; you do not want them to be mushy, or they will fall apart when you work. You may want to soak a few strips at time, using them when they are ready.

6 Working over the form, weave your base vertically and horizontally, gently lifting the ends of the stakes as necessary. If a stake does rip, try to reform the paper; add extra water to the ends, overlap them slightly, then press them together to adhere the fibers. For variation, you can weave strands of other fibers between your stakes. The basket in the photo, for instance, has strands of metallic-gold thread woven in.

7 Once the base is woven, weave the sides. Weave as you would for any basket (except for the fact that you are weaving upside down). Tuck the ends of each weaver under a stake, pressing the stake and the ends together. When the basket is woven, use your hands to gently press the basket all over. Make the stakes even with the rim of the bowl by ripping them or cutting them with a craft knife. If you desire, you can also leave the stakes long and uneven.

8 Allow the basket to air dry. Avoid rapid drying; this prevents the fibers from adhering. At this point you can remove the basket from the form. Or, you can apply acrylic gloss medium to make the basket stronger and water resistant. If you want to use the medium, dry the basket and keep it on the form. Using a brush, apply a coat of medium to the outside, and allow to dry. Gently remove the basket from the form, peeling away the plastic wrap. Then apply a coat of gloss medium to the inside of the basket, and allow to dry.

9 You can embellish your basket by gluing on beads or charms, or by attaching items with wire or waxed linen thread.

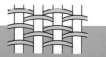

35

Random-Weave Basket with Natural Materials

Noted basket maker Carol Stangler has provided the following instructions for making a random-weave basket, which offer many possibilities when working with alternative materials.

Designer: **CAROL STANGLER**

"Random weave is an off-loom, nontraditional weaving style in which each element is both warp and weft. Typically, random-weave basketry consists of making a framework with vines, then weaving in more vines and other natural materials in a free-form fashion until the walls are layered, textured, and strong. The result is a sculptural, contemporary basket, so organic it appears to have woven itself.

Grapevines are a good choice for random weave, as they have the tensile strength to maintain a good, spherical form. Harvest grapevines in winter from cultivated or wild-growing plants. Collect long, flexible runners, thicker vines for the frame and thinner vines for the weavers. Work with them immediately, or store in a sheltered outdoor area, away from direct sunlight. Some varieties of grape will remain usable for up to six weeks.

When making your random-weave basket, try not to be too attached to a predetermined shape. Grapevines can be hard to control, so it's best to just "go with the flow" and let the basket determine its own form. Remember, your basket doesn't necessarily have to sit upright; a basket that lies on its side or leans into a corner can have a charm of its own."

MATERIALS

Grapevines for frame
Grapevines, dyed reed, strips of bark, seed pods, and bamboo branches for weaving into frame

TOOLS

Pruning shears
Twist-ties

INSTRUCTIONS

1 Form the rim (opening) of the basket. Choose a long, flexible grapevine. Find the approximate middle, and loop the two ends around to form a circle about 9 inches (22.5 cm) in diameter (see figure 1). As shown in figures 2 and 3, secure the opening by wrapping end B around the circle, then do the same with end A.

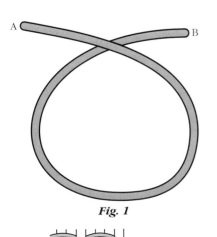

Fig. 1

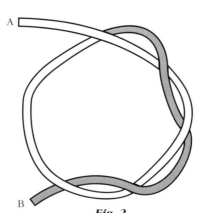

Fig. 2

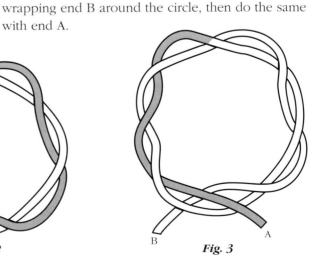

Fig. 3

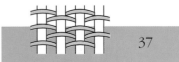

2 Form the initial depth and shape of the basket. As shown in figure 4, take vine end A, bring it down below the rim approximately 18 inches (45 cm), then back up to the rim, using enough vine to measure approximately 18 inches (45 cm) across. After you bring the vine up to the outside of the rim, bring it over the rim and then out again, wrapping the rim until you come to the end of the vine. Either secure the end between the vines of the rim, or let the end stick out to clip off later.

3 As shown in figure 5, take vine end B, bring it down below the rim and intersect it with vine A at the base of the basket. Secure with a twist-tie and bring the vine up to the outside of the rim. Wrap the vine around the rim, just as you did with vine A. Now you have the rudimentary framework of the basket.

4 You are now ready to make the walls of the basket, refine its shape, and strengthen the rim. You do this by adding many vines until a pleasant shape and a strong framework develop. To add vines, turn the basket upside down with the rim resting on the surface of a table. Lay the middle of a vine across the framework, then use a twist-tie to tie it to the intersecting vines (see figure 6).

5 As shown in figure 7, take vine ends C and D and wrap it around the basket, twist-tying at every point where it intersects with another vine. If it comes up to the outside of the rim, bring it around to the inside of the rim and back out again. Twist-tie if necessary. Continue laying the vine onto the framework and twist- tying until you run out of vine. The vine can end anywhere along the wall or tucked into the rim. Use the vines to break the big spaces into smaller spaces. Remember to keep the direction of the vines random, as opposed to organized verticals and horizontals. Continue to add and twist-tie more vines until the spaces between the intersecting vines are approximately 2 x 2 inches (5 x 5 cm), and the basket frame feels sturdy (see figure 8).

6 Now weave thinner vines, reed, pods, bamboo branches, and strips of bark over and under the vines of the frame as shown in figure 9. There is no need to use twist-ties when you do this. Continue adding as many weavers as possible since this weaving holds the basket together.

7 When the spaces between vines and other materials are very small, and the wall is thick and sturdy, remove the twist-ties. Clip or tuck in the ends.

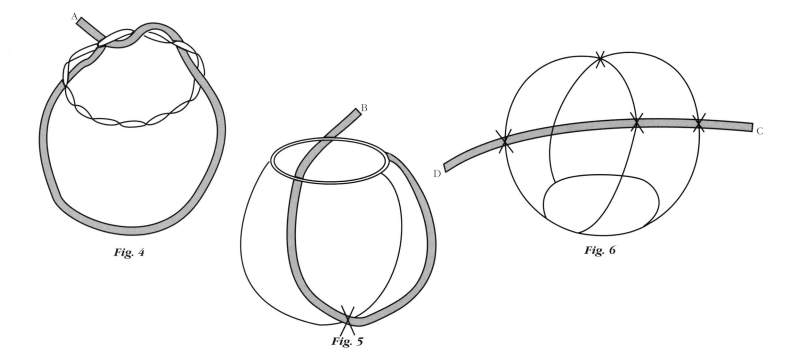

Fig. 4

Fig. 5

Fig. 6

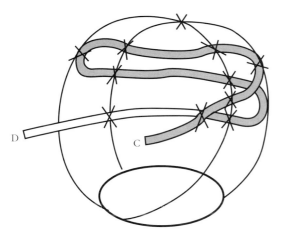

Fig. 7

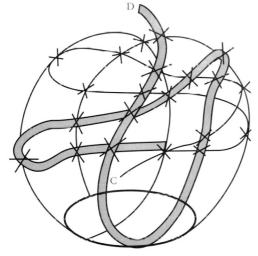

Fig. 8

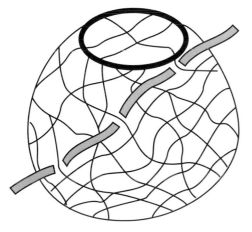

Fig. 9

Additional Materials

Here is a list of additional natural materials to use when making a free-form basket. You can also experiment with making your form from nylon clothesline, wire cable, or other ropes or cords that have a similar tensile strength to grapevine; then use natural or alternative materials for the weavers.

Vines for Framework

Honeysuckle
Kudzu (split or whole)
Wisteria
Greenbriar (remove thorns)

Materials for Weavers

Bark

Birch and River Birch
Tulip Poplar
Ash
Mulberry
Basswood
Hickory
Cedar
Hemlock

Pods

Locust
Catalpa
Trumpet Vine

Seed Stalks

Date Palm

Roots

Mulberry
Spruce Pine

Dried Plant Materials

Leaves of
Iris
Cattail
Yucca
Gladiolus
Philodendron

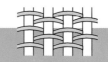

Plaiting Basics

WHILE PLAITING IS considered weaving, it has one distinguishing factor that places it in a separate category. Plaiting is always woven of elements (the warp and weft) that are alike; each approximately the same weight, the same thickness, the same width, and the same flexibility.

You can plait horizontally or vertically over upright elements using a separate weaver. This will create a traditional straight weave as shown in figure 1. Or, you can plait diagonally (on the bias) by weaving the elements at right angles to each other as shown in figure 2. Hexagonal plaiting, an open-work weave which uses a slightly different technique, is described later in this section.

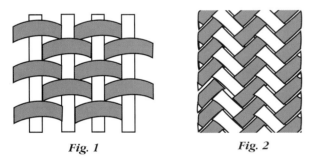

Fig. 1   *Fig. 2*

Since plaiting developed where soft grasses and large leaves are plentiful, plaited baskets rely on the tension between two like elements to hold them together and give them shape. Because the traditional materials used in plaiting are softer than wooden strips and vines, plaiting creates baskets that are softer (and often less sturdy for carrying heavy loads) than a woven basket. You can find many new materials for plaiting. Any soft material that is already in strips or can be easily cut into strips works well. Great projects can be made with paper, cardboard, ribbons, carpet webbing, plastic strapping material, and even old inner tubes.

You'll find that plaiting two like materials can be frustrating at first. The material tends to flop in all directions while you are turning up the sides (in straight plaiting) or making your corners (in diagonal plaiting). You also need to be constantly aware of adjusting the tension between the elements as you work. Don't be discouraged. Eventually you'll develop "smart hands," which is a tactile sense that comes with a little experience.

MEASURING

Before you begin, you must first determine the length of the elements. As for a woven basket, you can determine the lengths for straight plaiting by starting with the basket's finished dimensions (see page 10). Use the same formula, base + height + height, to get the measurements you will need. If you are planning on tucking in the ends rather than adding a rim after straight plaiting, you will need to figure on adding approximately 6 inches (15 cm) to the length of each strip (3 inches [7.5 cm] for each side). This is just an estimate; you may need to add more for your design.

Since diagonal plaiting is created by interweaving the elements at right angles to each other without using separate weavers, you will need extra length for each element when working this technique. Once you determine the length for the elements using the formula above, add approximately one-third more of that measurement to each element. Working at right angles also requires that you must start a diagonal plaited basket by interweaving the same number of vertical and horizontal elements.

When you are plaiting, you want the elements to lie next to each other without spaces in between (see figure 3). This helps create the tension that holds the basket together.

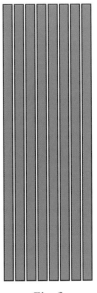

Fig. 3

WEAVING THE BASE

Whether you are making a basket using straight or diagonal plaiting, you will begin the baskets the same way. Lay the elements on a flat surface, and interweave them as you would when starting a woven basket with a woven bottom (see *Weaving the Base* on page 11). Make sure the elements lie close to each other without leaving spaces in between. True the

bottom (page 12), adjusting the vertical and horizontal strips to even the ends and to square the base. Using a pencil or marker, mark each corner on both the vertical and horizontal elements; then if they shift, you can always move them back into position (see figure 4).

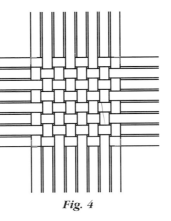

Fig. 4

Once you've trued the base and marked the corners, place clamps at the corners to hold the base together in preparation for turning up the sides. Depending on the materials you are using, you can use spring-type clothespins, small clamps, or micro alligator clips. When you are working with very soft material, you may need a little extra help in holding the base together. To do this, use one very thin, long strip of like material, fold it in half, then pair twine (see page 67) around each element; this effectively locks the woven base in place.

STRAIGHT PLAITING

This technique is very similar to making woven baskets with rigid stakes or spokes. Once you weave the base, you will turn the elements upright and weave around them with a separate weaver. The upright elements will most likely not have enough body to stand on their own, and the weavers will be similar to, or the same as, the upright elements in their degree of body. When you are at this stage, you will immediately understand the concept of plaiting—that the tension between the weavers and the upright elements holds the basket together.

If you've never plaited before, you may have difficulty working the first few rows. Since you are establishing the tension between elements at this point, everything will seem to be going everywhere all at the same time. Use as many clamps, clips, or clothespins as you need to hold the elements together. You may find it helpful to plait over a form that approximates the shape of the basket you are making. Have patience, and keep weaving; eventually the basket will begin to take shape and stand on its own.

Because you will have an even number of upright stakes, you will need to use a new weaver for each row. (Remember to overlap the end over the starting point by four stakes as explained in *Weaving the Sides* on page 13.) If you wish to weave around the basket without stopping and starting for every row (a continuous weave), you will need to fashion an odd number of stakes. As for a woven basket, simply cut one of the upright elements in half lengthwise to the base to get an uneven number.

Once you've completed weaving the basket, you can finish it by adding a lashed rim and handles (if desired) as described in *Making a Rim and Adding Handles* on page 13. Before adding the rim, even up the top edge of the basket by turning and folding the inside elements to the outside, and the outside elements to the inside; there's no need to tuck them in. Trim the ends so they will not protrude from the edge of the rim.

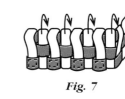

Fig. 5

A more traditional method of finishing plaited baskets is to fold the elements over, either to the outside or the inside (see figures 5 to 7), tucking them into the first available row of weaving, which is usually the third row from the top. (Some basketmakers describe this as "tucking down the throat.")

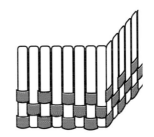

Fig. 6   *Fig. 7*

DIAGONAL PLAITING

Also called bias plaiting, diagonal plaiting is worked by weaving the elements at right angles to *each other*. You will *not* use separate weavers. This interweaving technique requires more length from each element to get the height you need for the basket. Use the formula base + height + height to calculate the length, then add one-third more of that measurement to each element. In order to weave at right angles, you will

always need to use the same number of vertical and horizontal elements.

Start a diagonal-plaited basket the same way as for a straight-plaited basket. As shown in figure 8, make a mental note of points A, B, C, and D on the woven bottom. These points will become the corners of the basket.

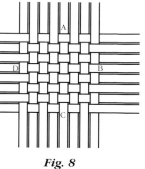

Fig. 8

Starting on any side of the square, divide the elements in half (at either point A, B, C, or D), then fold one-half of the elements over the other as shown in figure 9. Begin weaving in both directions as shown in figure 10—this is your first row. Continue weaving until you've woven all the elements as shown in figure 11, which will complete your first corner. Remember to use clamps, clothespins, or clips as needed to help keep the woven elements together. Repeat on all four sides of the square.

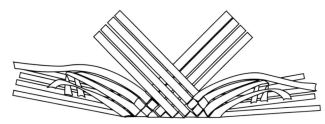

Fig. 9

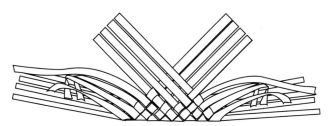

Fig. 10

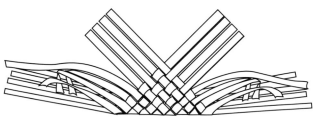

Fig. 11

As you work, the elements of one corner will naturally overlap the next. When they do, just weave them together. Continue weaving the elements until there are no more to weave. When you are finished, take time to adjust the spacing and tension between elements as needed.

To finish off, you can apply a rim (see page 13). However, the more traditional (and more interesting) way of finishing a diagonal-plaited basket is to tuck the ends in, which creates either a jagged edge or a flat edge as shown in figures 12 and 13.

Fig. 12   **Fig. 13**

When you finish weaving, you'll notice that the ends of the elements are still overlapping. To make a jagged edge, find a side where the elements are all going over one. Start with any two elements that cross, as in figure 14. Fold the inside element toward the outside and tuck it into its same weaving, as shown in figure 15. Now do the same with the other element, as shown in figure 16. Repeat this around the edge of the basket.

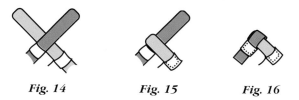

Fig. 14   **Fig. 15**   **Fig. 16**

To make a straight edge, begin by finding two elements that cross as in figure 14. Fold both ends over toward the outside as shown in figure 17, then tuck the ends into the opposite weave as shown in figure 18. Repeat this around the edge of the basket.

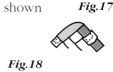

Fig.17

Fig.18

HEXAGONAL PLAITING

Though the open weave of hexagonal plaiting looks delicate, it is a strong weave that is used for chair seats. As with straight and diagonal plaiting, hexagonal plaiting is woven from like elements. However, rather than using softer elements, hexagonal plaiting works best with materials that have slightly more body to them, such as plastic strapping tape, laminated papers, heavyweight watercolor paper, cardboard, flexible barks, stiffened fabric and ribbons, or webbing.

To make a hexagonal basket, you first weave the base, then turn the elements up to weave the sides. To find the length of each element, follow the same procedure used for diagonal-plaited baskets as described on page 40. In hexagonal plaiting, the elements do not lie close to each other; therefore, the number of elements you use will be less than those used for a straight or diagonal-plaited basket.

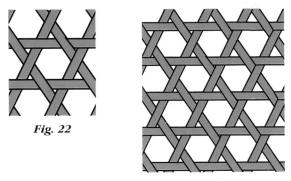

Fig. 22

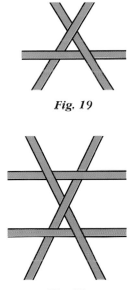

Fig. 19

Fig. 20

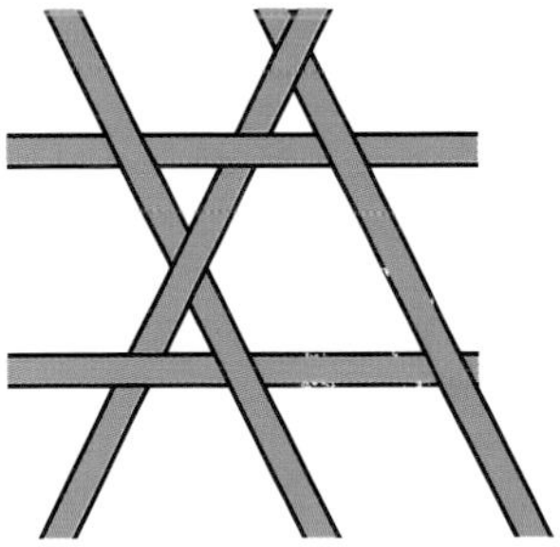

Fig. 21

To begin your bottom weave, take three elements and arrange them as shown in figure 19. Depending on the size of the material, use clamps, clothespins, micro-mini alligator clips to secure the outer corners of the triangle made by the three elements. Next, introduce a fourth element as shown in figure 20, moving the clamps to the outer four corners. Add a fifth element as shown in figure 21, again moving the clamps to the outer corners. Finally, add the sixth element as shown in figure 22. Continue adding elements in this same order, moving and adding clamps accordingly, until your base is the size desired. Adjust the elements as you work, keeping the space between them the same as shown in figure 23.

Fig. 23

When your base is complete, turn the elements upright. You'll notice that some elements point to the right and some to the left. You will be using a new weaver for each row following the start-stop method. Make sure you figure enough length for each weaver to allow for the overlapping of the ends. Begin weaving the first row by passing the weaver over all left-pointing elements and under all the right-pointing elements. Each row is woven this way. Continue weaving until the sides are as tall as needed.

To finish, you can bend the elements over the top row of weaving and add a lashed rim (page 13), cutting the ends of the elements once you complete the lashing. Or, you can create a jagged edge by folding the ends of each pair over the other (one to the front, one to the back), creasing the ends before tucking them into the weaving, as shown in figure 24.

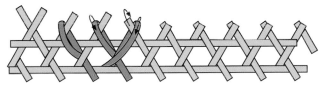

Fig. 24

Newspaper Basket

Designer Polly Harrison believes that making a simple basket from newspaper provides the maker with an immediate result of their recycling efforts. If you don't have newspaper handy, try wallpaper, gift wrap, paper sacks from the grocer, or whatever might find its way to you.

Designer: POLLY HARRISON

MATERIALS

12 (or so) full-size sheets of newspaper
Masking or cellophane tape
White craft glue
Acrylic polymer

TOOLS

6 to 8 clothespins or large paper clips
Scissors
Disposable foam brushes

INSTRUCTIONS

1 Open one sheet of newspaper and fold it in half from top to bottom. Fold it in half again, running your fingertips along the fold to make it even. Fold twice more until you have a strip approximately 1 inch (2.5 cm) wide. Note: It is very natural to want to fold the sheets from left to right as a newspaper page is read, but this will make shorter strips. Secure the ends of the folded strip with tape. Fold all remaining strips in this way.

2 Begin the base of the basket by placing three strips side by side with their ends even. Weave four strips in an under one, over one pattern across the center of the other three. Make sure they are snug against each other with no space in between. Clip clothespins in each corner.

3 To weave the sides, take the end of a new strip and begin to weave it into any side next to the base. Using another clothespin, clip the end in one of the corners. Take the other clothespin off the other corner and pin it to the new strip. Fold this new strip up after it is woven, and begin to weave it around the second side. Secure it with the re-pinned clothespin. Continue until you have circled the base. You should have enough of the strip left to overlap the beginning with the end. From this point, take each clothespin off one at a time and replace it immediately or your basket will fall apart.

4 For the next row, fold the stakes up on the side you are working on so you can see the weaving pattern. Weave a new strip into the stakes and clip with a clothespin. Continue weaving this strip until it overlaps. Remember to keep the pins on, taking them off only one at a time to replace the pin on the newly added strip. The basket will be stronger if you alternate adding strips on opposite sides of the basket. Make sure the weaving pattern is consistent, and that no strip has gone over two strips. Add the third strip, and weave.

5 Add the rim. Notice that some vertical strips are on the inside of the basket and others are on the outside. Fold all the inside strips over the top layer and down on the outside of the basket, then secure with clothespins. Let the outside strips stand straight up. Take a new strip, and overlay it on the strips you have pinned down; one at a time, take a pin off, lay the strip, then clip the pin back securely until this rim strip overlaps.

6 Fold a triangle in the end of any strip that is sticking up, then fold it over the rim strip, and weave it down into the next row of weaving below. Pull the end of the strip to tighten the basket. The ends will stick out; do not cut them. Continue until all the outside strips around the rim are woven. Note: This process is double weaving; if you look closely at the rim, you will see two layers. If you want to make a handle, go on to steps 7 and 8; if not go to step 9.

7 For a handle, take a new strip that has been folded in half, and weave the two ends of this handle-strip down next to the two center strips that are across from each other on the short sides of the basket. Adjust the length of the handle by working the ends up or down. When the handle is as long as desired, apply glue to the center strips and clip them to the handle with a clothespin. Add additional strips in the same way until the handle is as thick as desired.

8 To make the handle strong, use masking tape to secure the handle in several places. To wrap the handle, take another newspaper strip, and place the end at a diagonal between the handle and the rim. Glue the strip in place, holding it with a clothespin. Wrap the strip around the layers of the handle, dabbing glue on the strip as you wrap. If the strip is not long enough, overlap another strip to make it longer, tucking the ends so they will not show. Glue the end of the wrapping strip into the inside of the rim and handle on the other side.

9 Remove any clothespins. Separate the two layers of the rim, put a dot of glue between them, and secure with clothespins. Using scissors, closely trim off any of the ends that are sticking out; do not try to weave them further. Let the glue dry a few minutes, take the clothespins off, and you have your basic basket.

10 Exposure to air makes newspaper break down. To seal the newspaper, paint the basket with white glue or polymer. First paint the inside, handle, and outside. Let dry, smoothing any drips, and then paint the bottom. You could actually use any type of paint to decorate the finished basket.

VARIATIONS

You can make any shape you want by varying the number of strips in the base. If the basket gets too large for one strip to weave around it, overlap another strip, glue it in place, and keep going. If you get ambitious and want to work on a really big basket, you might think about giving the basket additional strength at important places by inserting wood splits, metal mini-blinds, or plastic strips inside the folded newspaper strips.

Why Not Newspaper?

Polly Harrison shares her thoughts on transforming this humble material.

Newspaper is one of the most highly underrated materials for making art. Even though we're quick to grab a sheet or two to wipe up a mess, wad it up, stuff it, shred it, cover it up with paint or plaster, or hide it with papier-mache, we seldom consider it as a primary material for making art.

Newspaper is free, it is sterile, and it is often very beautiful. Sports pages from Argentina are printed on pink tissue-thin shiny paper. One of my favorites is the "Nikkei News" from Japan, which I obtain from an Asian grocer who discards out-of-date issues.

Bias-Plaited Flapped Pillow

Designer Jackie Abrams says, "Once you know the technique, you can vary the size of the basket or the opening, create different color patterns, and do different tucks. Have fun while you experiment!"

Designer: **JACKIE ABRAMS**

MATERIALS

140# watercolor paper, half of a 22 x 30 inch
(56 x 76 cm)sheet
Acrylic paints in colors of your choice
Artist's polymer in matte or gloss finish

TOOLS

Disposable sponge brushes
Manual pasta machine, or, utility knife
and straightedge
20 to 30 micro alligator clips without teeth
Small pair of scissors
Small awl or screwdriver
Bone folder or large knitting needle

INSTRUCTIONS

Finished dimensions: 8 x 8 x 4 inches
(20 x 20 x 10 cm)

1 Paint both sides of the paper. One side becomes
the inside of the basket, the other side becomes
the outside. For this project I painted a solid color on
one side. On the other side, I used a sponge-painting
technique to dab on several layers of different color
paint, then spatter-painted the final layer.

2 The basket is woven with 24 weavers over 24
weavers; each weaver is 22 inches (56 cm) long.
To make the strips, cut your paper into three pieces,
each 5 inches (12.5 cm) wide and 22 inches (56 cm)
long. Carefully run the pieces through the pasta
machine. You'll get the necessary 48 weavers, plus a
few extras for any needed mending. If you do not
have a pasta machine, use a utility knife and straightedge to cut strips ¼ inch (.6 cm) wide and 22 inches
(56 cm) long.

3 Weave the base. Begin by weaving eight weavers
(four over four) using an over one, under one
pattern. Even up the ends of the weavers and mark
the center of the base. Continue to add weavers
equally all the way around. In plaiting, tension is
important; all weavers must be equidistant from each
other in all directions. A good way to tell if your tension is correct is to pay attention to the empty spaces;
each space should be squared and the same size,
approximately ¹⁄₁₆ inch (.15 cm). Continue to adjust the
tension as necessary.

4 Weave the base until it measures 5½ inches (13.8
cm) square. Use clips at each corner and at
every few weavers along the sides to hold the base in
shape. As shown in figure 1, locate each A and B
weaver; they are the
center weavers of each
side. Mark them by
putting clips halfway up
the sides of each A and
B weaver. This is impor-
tant!! These weavers
become the corners of
your base, and it's very
easy to lose track of
them once you start
weaving the sides.

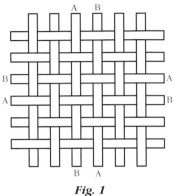

Fig. 1

5 Make a corner.
Starting on any
side, use two center
weavers (A and B), and
cross the one that is
under (B) over the one
that is over (A). This creates a bottom corner.
Keep the corner taut (no
space) as you weave it.

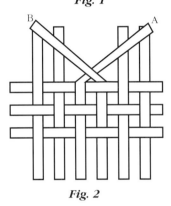

Fig. 2

6 Weave the side above the corner. Continue plaiting over one, under one on all the weavers
above the corner until you get an inverted-V woven
shape (a triangle). As you weave, the empty spaces
(see step 3) should be the same size as the ones on
the base. Move the clips as you weave to hold the
weaving in place. It is often easier to weave two
weavers at a time. Repeat this on each side of the base
until you have four corners and four woven triangles.
All the long weavers should be woven into each other.
Adjust all tensions.

7 Shape the shoulders.
There are now four
unwoven V-shapes, located
above the center of each side
of the base. Starting with any
V, gently push the woven sections together. Each unwoven
weaver will have a partner. As
shown in figure 3, one of the pair (B) will come over

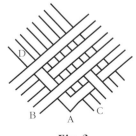

Fig. 3

the last woven weaver (D). Its partner (C) will come, on the opposite side, from underneath. This pattern will alternate with each pair.

8 Following figure 4, start at the bottom point of the triangle (A), and cut the weaver (B) so its end lays on top of D. Weave its partner (C) over the cut edge, and follow the over, under, over weaving pattern, laying C on top of its partner B. Do not cut the ends; leave them long for adjusting later.

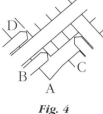

Fig. 4

NOTE: For easier threading, cut the ends of the weavers that are being woven on top of another at an angle. If necessary, use a small awl or screwdriver to lift the stakes to create a space.

9 Thread the next four partners in the same way. Keep the first ones relatively loose until all of them are woven. Then gently tighten so that the woven sections pull together. Remember to leave the same small square of empty space between the rows as in step 3. Repeat on all four shoulders. Adjust all tensions, and clip off the long ends of the weavers close to the weaving.

10 Fold the flaps. You now have four woven triangles with seven unwoven weavers in each direction. Gently fold the first triangle back over the woven basket. Using a bone folder or the tip of the knitting needle, score the strips before folding. Weave the ends of the weavers back into the basket, under one or more rows of weaving. Keep them a little loose until you've tucked in all four flaps.

11 Adjust the flaps and weaving so that the opening is square and the weaving tension is even. Clip the ends of the weavers. You can cut them flush with the weaving, or at a more decorative angle. For strength and protection, dilute the polymer with a little water and apply it to your basket.

Working with Paper

Designer Jackie Abrams specializes in making baskets from paper. Here are a few of her tips for working with this material.

Selecting Papers

Many papers will work for your baskets. Watercolor paper in a 140# weight, or some of the stiffer printmaking papers, have good body for weaving and will provide the most success. Experiment! A common paper size is 22 x 30 inches (56 x 76 cm).

Painting the Paper

You can paint the paper using one or several of the multitude of surface design/painting techniques. There is a wide variety of tools, including brushes, rollers, sponges, and stamps. I prefer acrylic paints; they are waterproof, fast-drying, and don't fade.

Cutting Paper

To make ¼-inch (.6 cm) strips, cut your paper using a manual pasta machine. (In pasta language, ¼ inch (.6 cm) equals fettucine.) When cutting other sizes, you'll get the best results using a utility knife and a straightedge. If you are cutting painted paper in a pasta machine, the paint must be thoroughly dry before cutting. Do not use your pasta machine for food preparation once you've used it to cut painted paper.

Weaving Paper

If you are used to working with reed, ash, or another heavier basket material, you will need to adjust your fingers to paper. Don't pull the paper, just place it. You can mend it if it rips, but it's really easier to just be more gentle as you go along. If a weaver does rip, place a new weaver on top of the old weaver. Overlap four spokes with both ends hidden.

Tools

Micro-mini alligator clips without teeth are great for holding the paper in place as you weave. You can't have too many. Find them where electronics are sold.

Laminated-Wrapper Hanging Basket

Take advantage of the colorful sparkle from foil wrappers to make this charming little envelope basket. Collect as many wrappers as you can, laminate them, then cut the laminated sheet into strips for diagonal plaiting.

Designer: **SYLVIA WHITE**

MATERIALS

Multicolored laminated paper
Raffia or yarn, one piece approximately
   3 yards (2.75 m) long
Silver gift-wrap cord, ⅛ inch (.3 cm) in diameter

TOOLS

Scissors
Clothespins
Small clips
Blunt needle with a large eye to fit cord
Hole punch that makes ⅛-inch (.3 cm) holes

INSTRUCTIONS

Finished dimensions: 7 x 5 inches (17.5 x 12.5 cm)

1 Laminate the paper. Collect candy wrappers, foil from butter, tea bags, envelopes, or other colored labels. Arrange them in a single layer, cutting the pieces if necessary, to fit next to each other. (I like to scatter the pieces randomly, or sometimes take advantage of the words on a label.) Place the pieces in a single layer in a 12⅛ by 18 inches (31 x 45 cm) lamination envelope (menu size). Be careful to avoid overlapping the labels or the lamination will separate. Following operating instructions, run the sheet through the laminator. (Most copy shops have laminating machines.)

2 After laminating the paper, cut it into 24 strips, each ½ inch (1.3 cm) wide by 18 inches (45 cm) long. Cut a 20-inch (50 cm) length of the silver cord.

3 Using the strips, straight plait in a plain-weave pattern (over one, under one) to make a woven square measuring 12 x 12 inches (30 x 30 cm). Center the strips, evening their ends, and adjust the tension. You can hold the square together by placing clothespins at the corners, or fold the piece of raffia or yarn in half and pair twine around the individual stakes around the edges of the square.

4 Turn the woven square so it is diamond-shaped. Use a pencil to draw a guideline horizontally in the middle of the diamond from the left point of the diamond to the right point. Instead of starting your diagonal plaiting on one of the sides, start plaiting on the corner facing you (the bottom point of the diamond.) Diagonal plait all ends, all the way around. If needed use small clips to hold the plaiting together as you work. Notice that the guideline becomes the fold at the bottom of the envelope.

5 Continue weaving until the sides are 5 inches (12.5 cm) high, or approximately seven diamonds counting straight up from the fold. Finish by making a straight edge as described and shown in figures 17 and 18 on page 42. Trim any excess ends.

6 Add the rim. Using the hole punch, punch holes ⅜ inch (.9 cm) down from the top edge of the basket, spacing the holes approximately 1 inch (2.5 cm) apart. Lay a ½-inch (1.3 cm) strip against the outside of the basket with the top edge of the strip flush to the top edge of the basket. Using the needle and silver cord, use an overhand (blanket) stitch to lash the rim to the basket.

7 To finish, make a handy handle for hanging the basket. Once you have lashed all the way around, make a knot at the end of the cord, but do not cut it. Using approximately 5 inches (12.5 cm) of excess cord, count five holes along one side of the envelope and make another knot into the existing stitches. Tuck approximately 1 inch (2.5 cm) of the ½-inch (1.3 cm) rim strip behind the beginning of the lashed rim and trim any excess.

Film Basket

You can find strips of 35mm film negatives   Designer: **POLLY HARRISON**

at your local movie theater. The designer gleaned these from the trailers used to announce the coming attractions.

MATERIALS

    35mm film

TOOLS

    Scissors
    One sheet of foam core, approximately
       ¼ inch (.6 cm) thick
    Push pins
    Large paper clips

INSTRUCTIONS

1 Cut the film into 14 lengths, each approximately 24 inches (61 cm) long. Center four of the lengths on top of the foam-core sheet, evening their ends. Using an under one, over one pattern, weave four pieces across, giving you a cross shape with a woven center. Using push pins, pin the square at its corners.

2 Weave a new piece into one of the sides and secure it on the end with a large paper clip. Fold up the side and continue weaving this new piece around until it circles the base and overlaps where it began. Weave the other three strips, overlapping their ends. Tighten the basket by gently pulling the stakes up and the weavers around.

3 Weave the rim. Notice that there are some spokes on the inside of the basket and some on the outside. Fold the outside spokes to the inside and weave them down on the inside. You will go over two rows before weaving, but don't worry about it. Fold the inside spokes to the outside and weave them down into the basket.

4 Cut a triangle on the end of a new piece of film and weave it around the inside of the basket on the rim, over one, under one, to reestablish the weaving pattern. Repeat this step on the outside of the rim. Closely trim off any ends of film that are sticking out.

TIP

Make the rim and the base of your basket stronger. For the rim, weave another material over the top row before weaving the rim. You can use thin reed that's been painted black, metal blinds, cut strips of aluminum, or plastic strapping. Weaving the rim will hide whatever you use. For the base, cut a piece of clear plastic sheeting the size of the base, then use rivets to attach it at the corners.

Cone-Shaped Bowl

*By weaving half the basket
on a flat surface, designer
Jodi Bamford helps you*

Designer: Joni Bamford

*avoid working with the unruly weavers usually associated with
plaiting. Use three colors for a checkerboard pattern, or more
colors to create a graduated color scheme.*

MATERIALS

24 strips of stiff ½-inch (1.3 cm) paper tape,
each 18 inches (45 cm) long

18 strips, each ⅜ inch (.9 cm) wide by 6 inches
(15 cm) long. These could be cut from
photographs, stiff magazine pages, contrasting
paper tape, wallpaper, plastic tape, or stiff
ribbon. (Optional)

1 strip of stiff 1-inch (2.5 cm) paper tape,
approximately 24 inches (61 cm) long

White craft glue

TOOLS

Scissors
24 mini alligator clips or paper clips

INSTRUCTIONS

1 Note your design choices: To make a basket with
a three-way checkerboard design, choose three
different colors, cutting eight strips of each color.
(Figure 1 shows the layout scheme for working with
three colors to get this effect.) To make a basket with
a graduated color scheme, choose related colors or
shades, then cut multiples of three strips to make up
the total 24 strips (e.g., three light, six medium, six
darker, nine very dark = 24).

2 On a flat surface, lay out eight strips horizontally,
with each one touching the next. If necessary,
weight the sides down to keep the ends from curling.
Mark the center points of these strips. Mark the center
points of the remaining 16 strips. Place one strip to the
left of the center point of the horizontal strips. Using an
over one, under one pattern, weave the *bottom half* of
this strip vertically
across the horizon-
tal strips. In the
same way, weave
in another seven
strips to the left side
of this one, alternat-
ing the weave pat-
tern. Next,
following the same
process, weave in
the remaining eight
strips to the right of
the center point of

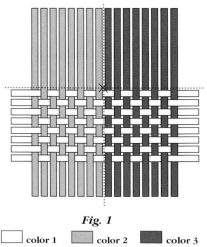

Fig. 1

☐ color 1   ▨ color 2   ▩ color 3

the horizontal strips. Note that all weaving is below the
center point of the vertical strips, as shown in figure 1.
Once all the strips are in place, push them up close to
one another, then use mini-alligator clips to clip each
corner to hold the rectangle together. Make sure there
are no gaps between the strips.

3 Begin forming the cone. With clips on all four
corners of the flat rectangle, take the two strips
on either side of point X (see figure 1) and cross them
at right angles, taking care to follow the over one,
under one weave. Clip the two in place. Then take the
two strips on either side of the first two, and weave
them across each other, then across the other two
strips as shown in figure 2. This will make a 2 x 2
square. Note that figure 2 is drawn to illustrate the
weaving pattern; when you weave the strips, make
sure that there are no gaps between them.

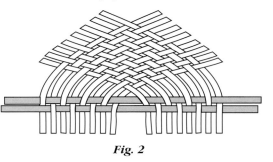

Fig. 2

4 From this point, it's easier to weave on the outside of the basket, with the point of the cone
facing you. Continue to weave strips from each side
across each other. If you are weaving with three colors, you will see the checkerboard design. As you
weave, move the clip each time to hold the strips in
place. Keep crossing the strips at right angles, over
one, under one, with no gaps between the strips.
When all the long ends of the strips are woven across
each other, clip the center of each long side to hold
the cone together.

5 *(Optional)* Before finishing the edges, you can
alter the design by weaving the narrower ⅜ by
6-inch (.9 x 15 cm) strips on top the existing weave.
To do this, keep all the clips in place from step 4. Start
to weave the narrower strips over the central three
strips first, then continue to weave outward. To help
you ease the narrower weavers through, use a narrow
piece of thin card with a pointed end to lift up the

already-woven paper strips. Adjust all the new weavers, tightening them up so no gaps show, and trim off any unwanted ends.

6 Finish the edges. To make the simple straight edge as shown in the photo on the basket to the left, begin by working from the outside of the cone. Hold two strips where they cross at a corner, then fold them down toward you so the strips are aligned along the edge of the basket. Over the edge strip, fold and tuck in all the strips to the right and left of the corner, they will alternately go over one and over two before tucking in. (See figure 3.) Repeat for the other two corners. To make the tucking in easier, cut or fold the end of each strip to make a point. For greater strength, continue to weave each strip across the basket as far as it will go.

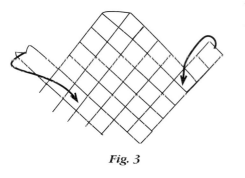

Fig. 3

7 To make the raised diagonal edge, as shown in the photo on the basket to the right, begin by finding the halfway point of each side. At one of those points, turn two adjacent strips across each other to make another corner. (Remember to keep the over one, under one weave in the right sequence.) Clip these two strips to hold them together. Then weave

the next strip on either side across to make a 2 x 2 square as you did in step 3. Move the clip to hold it in place. Repeat at the other two sides.

8 To finish the edge, you now need to unweave the points of the original sides. Unweave the strips back down to a diagonal row of crossing weavers that are in line with the three new corners. Place a clip where each pair crosses. Make sure that each pair of weavers is crossing at right angles. Fold an inner one over its partner to the outside of the basket. Then fold the partner over, again to the outside, to make a point as shown in figure 4. Put the clip back, and continue to work this way around the edge. Tuck each weaver down in turn, making sure that one weaver holds the next one in line, and continue to weave each one across the back of the basket, to strengthen it.

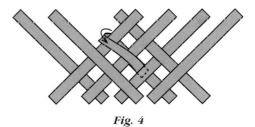

Fig. 4

VARIATIONS

You can make a small base to hold your cone basket upright. Roll the 1-inch (2.5 cm) paper tape into a small cylinder with a 1-inch (2.5 cm) diameter, and glue the overlapping ends. Apply glue to the edge of the base, then insert the cone, weighing it down if necessary until the glue dries. You can also let your cone basket sit on one of its sides as a display piece.

Hex Woven Strapping Tape Basket

The open hexagonal weave provides a perfect space for adding embellishments. The colorful small springs strung on wire fill the void perfectly. Shiny copper ribbon adds a touch of elegance to plain white strapping tape.

Designer: **SYLVIA WHITE**

MATERIALS

½-inch (1.3 cm) white polypropylene strapping tape*
24-gauge copper wire
½-inch (1.3 cm) copper-colored gift-wrap ribbon
Multicolored spring beads (available at bead stores)

TOOLS

Scissors
Needle-nose pliers

* Available at businesses or industries that ship large packages (e.g. printers, shippers) and also in large quantities from manufacturers of packaging, shipping, and warehouse products. The tapes are mostly in black, white, blue, and yellow. I usually buy 100 feet (30 m) from a local printer or mailing company. I have also used recycled strips from newspaper distributors.

INSTRUCTIONS

Finished dimensions: Base, 5½ inches (13.8 cm); height, 6 inches (15 cm); top diameter, 5½ inches (13.8 cm)

1 Cut the ½-inch (1.3 cm) white tape into 10 strips, each 24 inches (61 cm) long. Cut nine of these strips in half lengthwise, making 18 strips, each ¼ inch (.6 cm) wide; you will use these for weaving the body of the basket. You will use the remaining ½-inch (1.3 cm) white strip for the rim. From the copper ribbon, cut five strips, each 24 inches (61 cm) long.

2 Following the directions for hexagonal plaiting on page 42, lay and weave the strips until you have a hexagonally woven base that measures 5½ inches (13.8 m) in diameter; there should be three hexagonals on a side.

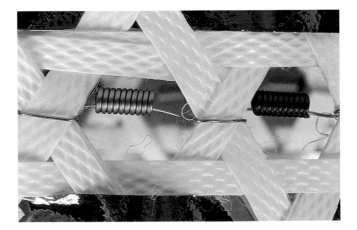

3 Turn the stakes up and shape the sides. Following the directions on page 43, use six strips and weave them in start-stop rows. When finished, you should have three Xs counting straight up from the base. The fourth X will become part of the rim.

4 To make the rim, lay the remaining white ½-inch (1.3 cm) strip on the outside of the top of the basket. Bend the ends of the upright weavers over the ½-inch (1.3 cm) strip, then tuck them into their matching weaver at the first opportunity.

5 To decorate with copper ribbon, start with the bottom row of parallel white strips and insert a copper ribbon into one of the hex openings. Weave it over and under the Xs around the basket, between the other parallel white strips. Leave enough ribbon to overlap the ends, and glue. Skip one row of parallel strips, then weave a copper ribbon in the next one; continue alternating rows and weaving until you have no more rows to weave. Next, turn the basket over and use a plain weave to fill in all the hexagonal openings at the bottom.

6 To add the springs and wire, first cut a piece of 24-gauge copper wire at least one-and-one-half times the circumference of the basket. Use the needle-nose pliers to wrap the wire around one of the Xs just above the bottom row of copper ribbon. Thread a spring bead on the wire and wrap the wire around the next X. Continue around in this way until you circled the basket. Finish by inserting the wire into the first loop you made in the row and twisting it closed. Circle the basket two more times with beads and wire, placing them between the copper ribbons.

Basket of Champions Necklace

*Put those bright wake-up colors on your cardboard cereal boxes to
use by weaving them into attractive pouch neck-
laces. Nicki Shaban, using a true designer's vision,
found beauty in an unlikely place to create this fanciful design.*

Designer: **NICKI SHABAN**

MATERIALS

Cereal box, at least 10 inches (25 cm) high
4-ply waxed linen thread in two colors, calling
    one color A, and the other color B
Acrylic varnish, water-base matte finish
Embellishments of choice,beads, charms, shells,
    and assorted fetishes

TOOLS

Manual pasta machine with fettuccine setting or
    attachment (suitable for making ¼-inch
    (.6 cm) noodles)
Craft knife
Ruler
Tape measure
Pencil
#18 tapestry needle
Small scissors (cuticle scissors work well)
Micro alligator clips, found in an electronics store
White glue
Small paintbrush or toothpick

INSTRUCTIONS

Finished dimensions: Height, 2⅝ inches (6.7 cm);
width, ⅜ inch (.9 cm); length, 1¾ inches (4.5 cm)

1 Cut out the colorful front panel from a cereal box.
Cut the panel in half vertically to get two rectangular pieces, each measuring approximately 10 x 4 inches
(25 x 10 cm). Using the pasta machine on the fettuccine
setting, or with a fettuccine attachment, insert the 4-inch
(10 cm) side of one of the rectangular pieces. Carefully
guide it through the machine, keeping it straight. Repeat
with the other rectangle. These 10 x ¼-inch (25 x .6 cm)
strips will be used for both the stakes and weavers. If
you do not have a manual pasta machine, cut the strips
by hand. First measure ¼-inch-wide (.6 cm) strips on the
back of the panel. Then, with a ruler as a straightedge,
use a craft knife to cut the strips.

58

2 Select six stakes from the strips. On the unprinted side, use a pencil to mark the center of each strip. Place one stake horizontally on the table with the unprinted side facing up. Place a second stake, unprinted side up, vertically on top of the first, lining up their center marks. Next, to each side of the central vertical stake, weave two vertical stakes using an under one, over one pattern.

3 Cut a 54-inch (1.4 m) length of waxed linen thread in color A. Fold the length in half, and pair twine (see page 62) over each individual stake, twining once around the base of the basket. Use the tapestry needle to pack the thread close to the base stakes. Do not cut the thread. Your base measurement should be approximately ⅜ x 1¾ inches (.9 x 4.5 cm).

4 Gently bend your stakes into an upright position, then continue to twine for three more rows. When completed, bring the ends of the thread to the inside of the basket. Using the tapestry needle, thread each end under a section of twining, then tie the two ends into a square knot, keeping the ends on the inside of the basket. Looking at the print on your stakes, decide which side will be the front of the basket.

5 Weave the sides. The basic pattern will be one row of start-stop plain weave, then two rows of twining. Plan to make all overlaps for the start-stop weave on the back of the basket which will lie against your body. To begin weaving, place a weaver to the outside of a stake that is under the horizontal base stake. Use a micro alligator clip to secure the weaver to the stake. Weave around using an over one, under one pattern. As you weave, use more clips to hold the row in place. Use the needle as a pick to pack the weaver as close as possible to the four rows of twining. End the row by overlapping by four stakes, then hiding the end behind the fourth stake.

6 Cut a 30-inch (76 cm) length of waxed linen thread in color B. Fold the length in half, and twine around the stakes for two rows. Bring the ends to the inside and tie them in a square knot. Continue to alternate weaving with twining. Also alternate the colors of waxed linen thread from color A to color B. When the sides are completed, you will have six rows of weaving, alternating with six sections of twining. The last row of the basket, before weaving the false rim, should be two twined rows of color A. Pack down all the rows with the tapestry needle.

7 Make your false rim by trimming a ¼-inch (.6 cm) weaver in half lengthwise. Weave the false rim. Cut the upright stakes that are on the inside of the basket even with the top of the false rim. Trim the outside stakes so they are ¼ inch (.6 cm) above the top of the false rim. Using a fine paintbrush or toothpick, apply glue to the unprinted side of the outside stakes. Then fold them to the inside of the basket, securing them with micro alligator clips until they are dry. Remove clips.

8 Fit and lash the rim. Place a ¼-inch (.6 cm) strip around the inner circumference of the basket, overlapping the ends in the back by ⅜ inch (.9 cm). Hold in place with clips, then repeat for the outer rim. The two overlaps should lie beside each other. Lay two pieces of waxed thread on top of the false rim, and between the inner and outer rim. Cut a 54 inch (1.4 m) length of thread in a color of your choice. Thread one end through the tapestry needle, and knot the other end, leaving a 2-inch (5 cm) tail. Below the rim, thread the lasher from the inside of the pouch to the outside, and whipstitch completely around the rims in one direction, then reverse direction to create a double lashing. When the lashing is complete, tie the lasher end and the 2-inch tail with a square knot, and trim.

9 Using a small brush, apply one or two light coats of varnish to the outside of your basket, allowing each coat to dry thoroughly before applying the next one. Let dry overnight.

10 Cut two pieces of waxed linen thread for the necklace. Attach the ends on the inside of the rim. Bead or knot as desired. Add embellishments of choice, and attach to the rim of your woven basket. Enjoy your wearable work of art!

Woven Paper Bag

What could be easier? By keeping the base of the bag intact, most of your work is done. Several coats of spray varnish will strengthen the paper, allowing you to use this woven bag as a unique display for dried arrangements or armfuls of wildflowers.

Designer: NANCY TAYLOR MCGAHA

MATERIALS

Two brown paper bags
Spray varnish in either matte finish or semi-gloss
Double-sided tape
White craft glue

TOOLS

Tape measure or ruler
Pencil
Craft knife
Scissors
Clothespins

INSTRUCTIONS

1 Measure around the bag to calculate the number of stakes you will need. (This will vary according to the size of your bag.) You want the stakes to be fairly wide and in proportion to the bag. The stakes for this project are approximately 1-1/2 inches (3.8 cm) wide.

2 Lay the bag on a flat surface. Using the ruler and pencil, lightly draw your cutting lines. Using the craft knife, cut along the lines from the base of the bag to 6 inches (15 cm) from the top. (Leaving the space at top makes weaving easier.)

3 Cut the second paper bag for your weavers. Cutting lengthwise, make each strip approximately 1-1/2 inches (3.8 cm) wide. You want your weavers to be the same width as the stakes.

4 Beginning at the bottom, weave a paper strip. You will be weaving start-stop, plain weave in an under one, over one pattern. To begin, use a clothespin to clip the end of the first weaver to the stake. Use double-sided tape to fix the weaver to the stake. Weave, then end the row by overlapping four stakes. Use double-sided tape to fix the end to the stake.

5 When you've completed the first row, open the bag fully, then prop it open with a large, lightweight object. Continue weaving and taping the ends until you reach the top. When you are finished, go back to all the taped ends and apply glue. Use clothespins to hold the ends in place while the glue dries.

6 When the glue is dry, fold the top of the bag over to the outside. Apply a light coat of spray varnish and allow to dry. Apply another light coat and allow to dry. Apply as many coats as needed to achieve the stiffness desired, allowing each coat to dry thoroughly before applying the next.

Recycled Cardboard Basket

Look around! By using what you have on hand, you can produce a basket from virtually nothing. Designer Peggy DeBell created this fanciful basket from a card-board box and bits and pieces from her other work. She plans on using it to store art materials—the handles make it easy to grab from a shelf.

Designer: **PEGGY DEBELL**

MATERIALS

Corrugated cardboard boxes (single ply)
Paint—any leftover house paint, textile paints,
    crayons, etc., will do
Webbing, old belt, or shaker tape (for handles)
Cotton clothesline
String
Beads
Rickrack

TOOLS

Long metal ruler, 36 inches (.9 m) long
Rotary cutting tool and cutting mat, or a utility knife
Disposable sponge brushes
Clothespins or small clamps
Hot glue gun and glue sticks
Awl
Scissors

INSTRUCTIONS

Finished dimensions: 14 x 7 x 5½ inches
(35 x 17.5 x 13.8 cm)

1 Choose a cardboard box and open it up so it lies flat. Make sure it is large enough; the strips you cut from it must be cut in one piece.

2 Cut the strips using the rotary cutting tool or a utility knife and the long metal ruler as a straightedge. Make each strip 2½ inches (6.25 cm) wide. Cut: four 29-inch (73.5 cm) lengths (the lengthwise stakes); eight 22-inch (56 cm) lengths (the widthwise stakes); three 51-inch (129.5 cm) lengths (the weavers); and two 46-inch (117 cm) lengths (the rim). Once the strips are cut, paint them on both sides in any color you choose. Allow to dry.

3 Mark the center point of the four 29-inch (73.5 cm) lengthwise strips, then lay them side by side. Lay four of the 22-inch (56 cm) lengths to the right of the center point of the lengthwise stakes, and four of the 22-inch (56 cm) lengths to the left of the center point.

4 Beginning with the center strips, and working your way toward the ends, weave your base in an over one, under one pattern. You want the weaving to be tight. To do this, fold the strips back on themselves as you weave so that each new strip will butt up against the previous one. Use clothespins to

hold the woven base in place. It should measure approximately 7 x 14 inches (17.5 x 35 cm). Print, paint, or draw as desired on both sides of the woven base, and let dry (see *Tips* below).

5 Fold the stakes up by creasing them at the base. Weave in the three 51-inch (129.5 cm) lengths. Each row is woven start-stop in an over one, under one pattern. Using your fingers, pack the rows tightly against each other. Use clothespins to hold the rows in place as you work.

6 When you've finished weaving the rows, cut the stakes flush with the last row of weaving and use clothespins or clamps on each stake to hold them in place. Gluing the outside stakes first, hot glue all stakes to the last row of weaving.

7 Cut two lengths of webbing for your handles. Position them where you want them, then hot glue the ends of the handles to the ends of the basket.

8 For your rim filler, paint or dye clothesline and place two rows side by side on top of the last row of weaving and the glued stakes. Hot glue in place. To make the rim, fit one of the 46-inch (117 cm) lengths of cardboard on the *inside* of the top row, overlapping the ends by 4 inches (10 cm). Then, starting to the right of the end of the inside rim's overlap, fit the other strip on the *outside*, again overlapping by 4 inches (10 cm). (The ends of the overlap look nice if they are mitered.) If desired, glue rickrack or trim on the rim.

9 In order for the lashing to pass through, use the awl to punch a hole in the space between each stake just below the rim (24 spaces). Lash on the rim, passing individual lengths of string through the holes, then tying them with square knots on the top of the rim. If desired, you can add beads to the ends of the string, or leave them hanging as a fringe.

TIPS: I used a real leaf to print on the cardboard in Step 4. To do this, just paint the leaf, turn it over onto the cardboard, and press with your fingers. The clothesline for the rim-filler and the strings for lashing were leftovers from my tie-dye work; the rickrack is from my sewing box.

Flat Woven Basket

By using materials found in a building-supply store, you can create this whimsical theme basket. You weave the twill on a flat surface using PVC tape, which is used by carpenters to edge furniture, then attach it to a hardware-cloth armature that allows you to shape the sides as you wish. Designer Mary Lee Fulkerson says, "After you learn the shaping technique, consider replacing the strips with woven fabric, knotless netting, or crocheted or knitted strips."

Designer: **MARY LEE FULKERSON**

MATERIALS

Hardware cloth in ½-inch (1.3 cm) mesh
PVC tape*
Spray paint in three to four colors of your choice
Cyanoacrylate glue or other strong glue
Felt-tip marker in bright color
Monofilament
Coated telephone wire**
Edging material, such as strips of artist canvas,
    upholstery fabric, webbing, etc.
Acrylic paint
Embroidery cotton
Spray acrylic in a matte finish

TOOLS

Wire cutters
Work gloves
Long metal ruler
Pruning shears
Masking tape
Clothespins
Long tapestry needle
Craft knife
Knitting needle, pencil, or dowel
Artist's paintbrush

* Used by carpenters to edge furniture, it comes in large rolls in ⅞- and 1-inch (2.2 and 2.5 cm) widths, and can be purchased at builders' supply stores. It can be spray-painted, needs no soaking, and is inexpensive! You can also use thick, smooth upholstery fabric for your plaited strips, treating them as you would the PVC tape.

** This comes wrapped inside an outer rubberized coating which you strip away. It is purchased by length, and comes in various colors.

INSTRUCTIONS

1 Choose a shape, then play with it. Figure 1 shows two possibilities: one for a triangular shape as featured in the photo, and one for a square shape. (Check Shereen LaPlantz's Twill Basketry for more shapes.) Whatever shape you choose, be sure you have a base! Then, determine the size of the finished basket. (I usually do this with a throw rug. With the center of the rug on a table, I grasp both ends and fold it upward to give me an idea of the approximate finished size.)

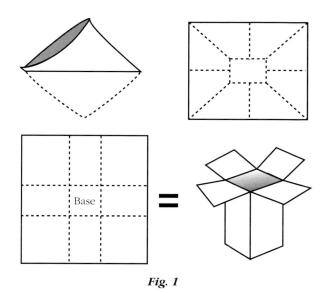

Fig. 1

2 Cut an armature (form). Using wire cutters and wearing gloves to protect your hands from the metal, cut a piece of hardware cloth into a square that is 2 inches (5 cm) smaller than the size you have determined for your finished basket.

3 Measure, and with pruning shears, cut strips of PVC tape 2 inches (5 cm) longer than the hardware-cloth square. Depending on the width of the PVC tape, cut enough strips to plait in both directions. Using the masking tape, tape all the cut strips vertically to an old cardboard box. In a well-ventilated area, spray paint the strips in swirls using different colors. Allow the paint to dry overnight.

4 Lay half of the painted strips on the table vertically in an even line, sides nearly touching. Tape the top of the strips to the table with masking tape. With the remaining strips, plait the tape in an over two, under two twill weave following this pattern: first row, over two, under two, etc.; second row, under one, over two, under two, over two, under two, etc.; third row, under two, over two, under two, over two, etc.; fourth row, over one, under two, over two, under two, etc. Repeat as necessary. Adjust the tension, then glue the ends of the strips, clipping them with clothespins until the glue is dry.

5 Shape the armature. Using the ruler and marker, measure and mark the fold lines on the square of hardware cloth. Measure accurately; you can't rebend hardware cloth. (If you are making a box shape, cut

away any extra hardware cloth as shown in figure 2.) Lay the ruler along your marked lines, and hold it firmly against the hard-ware cloth with one hand while folding the cloth upward with the flat of your other hand. Turn the cloth, hold the ruler, and fold, continuing in this way until you've folded all lines.

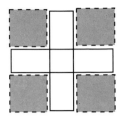

Fig. 2

6 Turn the armature upside down on the table. Arrange the plaited tape over the armature, painted side out. To secure the base to the armature, use the tapestry needle and monofilament to sew the tape to the armature at several places on the base.

7 Use lengths of telephone wire to attach the plaited form to the sides of the armature. Using a craft knife, slit the outer coating of the telephone wire to expose the inner wires. Cut the telephone wire into 14-inch (35 cm) lengths. From the outside of the plaited form, push an end of wire through a hole in the weave, then through a square in the hardware cloth. Next, take the wire around an adjacent square, then back out through the plaiting. Twist the wire tightly to hold, leaving the ends free as a design element. Attach wire in several places. To curl the ends of the wire, wrap the ends around a round form, such as a pencil or knitting needle, to shape.

8 Measure and cut the edging material; you want it to fold over one plaited row inside and outside. Paint the edging with acrylic paint in colors of your choice, and allow to dry. Arrange the painted tape around the glued edges. Using embroidery cotton in a

compatible color, use an overhand stitch to attach the edging to the plaiting (as you would lash a rim). Spray with a matte finish acrylic. The basket is complete. Use the basket it as is, or see the sidebar below for creating-a-theme basket as shown in the photo.

Create-a-Theme Basket

To make the theme basket you will need:

Polystyrene blocks (used for flower arranging)
White craft glue
Wooden dowels in varying diameters
Acrylic paint or spray paint
Round and ¼-inch (.6 cm) flat reed
    in various colors
Waxed linen thread
Coated telephone wire
Theme objects (themes can be games, sports, family, love, food, anything you wish!)
Excelsior, in colors of your choice

INSTRUCTIONS

Measure and cut polystyrene blocks to fit inside the basket. Glue a block to the inside bottom then stack the blocks in layers, gluing in between, until they are two-thirds up the side of the basket. Weight the blocks and allow to dry.

Arrange dowels at various angles inside the basket, pushing the dowels through the polystyrene, then cut the dowels at various heights. Remove the dowels, paint or spray paint, and let dry. Glue the dowel in the holes in the polystyrene and allow to dry.

Soak colored reed until flexible and twist around the dowels, attaching the reed with wire scraps or string until dry (as shown in figure 3), then arrange on dowels as you wish.

Now the fun part! With waxed linen and/or coated wire, attach theme objects to the dowels. When finished, hide the polystyrene by covering it with the colored excelsior.

Fig. 3

CONSIDER TWINING AS weaving with a twist. To twine, you use two or more weavers to encircle the stakes or spokes. When you use two weavers, known as *pairing or pair twining*, the weavers follow an alternate over-under weave which, when completed, surrounds the stakes or spokes, creating a distinctive twist between the stakes or spokes, as shown in figure 1.

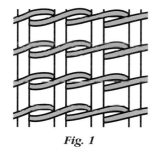

Fig. 1

When you use two weavers over an even number of stakes or spokes it is called a *chase weave*, since one weaver is always chasing the other as you work a continuous weave around the basket. When you use three or more weavers, it is known as waling. Like weaving, the pattern for a twined basket can be altered by using either an even or odd number of stakes or spokes.

For twining, you can use rigid elements for the stakes or spokes and more pliable elements for the weavers as you would for woven baskets. You can also use two fairly soft elements, since the encircling weavers create the tension that holds the stakes or spokes together. When using two softer elements, the basket may not stand on its own while you are weaving. Since this can be frustrating, you may find it helpful to twine your basket over a form, such as an inverted bowl.

The traditional materials used for the weavers in twining are willow or round reed. You can substitute a wide variety of new materials, such as twine, sisal, or hemp roping, wire, both coated and uncoated, plastic gimp, or leather lacing. Just keep in mind that the weavers always need to be fairly flexible, since this technique relies on your ability to manipulate the weavers around the stakes or spokes.

While you can make square twined baskets, the continuous round-and-round weaving rhythm of twining lends itself perfectly to making round and oval shapes. Since all the twining projects in this book make round baskets, this section will cover how to begin a round basket, turning up the sides, pairing, three-rod and four-rod waling, and finishes.

MEASURING

The traditional technique for creating twined baskets involves making the base separately, attaching the elements that will become the upright stakes to the finished base, then turning the attached elements up for weaving. This creates a sturdy basket capable of holding heavy loads. However, when working with new materials, you will most likely be creating baskets that do not need this degree of strength. You will find it easier to figure the upright elements as part of the base, then you can simply turn the elements up once the base is woven.

Following this technique, you will need to find the length for the base and the upright elements as you would for making a round woven basket (see page 11). First determine the approximate finished measurement of the basket you will be making. Then use the formula base + height + height to get the individual measurement you will need. Be sure to add additional length for finishing. There are many decorative borders used in twining, and the border you will use will determine any extra length you will need. The finished diameter of the basket, plus the spacing you desire between stakes, will determine the number of stakes to prepare.

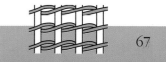

WEAVING THE BASE

A round base is created by first either laying half of the stakes crosswise on the remaining half, or by inserting half of the elements

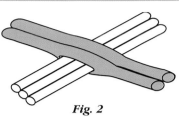

Fig. 2

crosswise into the remaining half (see figure 2), then lashing them together at their point of intersection.

The material you use for your upright stakes will determine whether you will lay the elements on top of each other or insert them. Be aware that thicker materials will work much better if you can insert the elements into each other, since this will make a flatter bottom that will prevent the completed basket from rocking. Of course if you are working with materials that cannot be cut or are too fragile for cutting, you will need to lay them on top of each other.

Once you've either inserted the elements or laid them on top of each other, a simple lashing technique using pair twining is all you will need to hold them together. Begin by taking a long piece of weaver and folding it in almost in half (you want one end slightly longer than the other). Wrap the fold around the stakes, as shown in figure 3. Bring the end of the weaver that is in back to the front, placing it over the next group of elements; then bring the weaver that is in front to the back, placing it under this same group of elements, as shown in figure 4. Continue in this way, alternating over and under the groups of elements, until you have completed several rounds. For a strong, secure base, make sure you pull the weavers tight against the elements as you work around them.

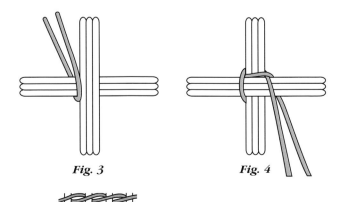

Fig. 3   *Fig. 4*

Once you have completed several rounds of the lashing, you are ready to open out the stakes to create the round base. Begin by separating the first stake from its group, then pair twine around it by manipulating the ends of the weavers under and over it, as shown in figure 5. To help you keep track of subsequent rounds, you may find it helpful at this stage to mark the first stake with a twist tie or piece of yarn. Continue pairing around the individual stakes, adjusting the distance between stakes to create an even distance between them, as shown in figure 6. You may need to add extra stakes to achieve the spacing you desire. Add the extra stakes as needed by inserting them through the weaving and into the lashing, while you continue to pair.

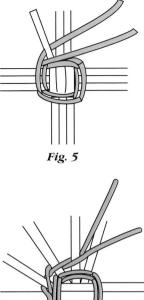

Fig. 5

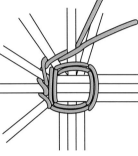

Fig. 6

Continue working around the base, as shown in figure 7, until it is the diameter you desire. If you need to

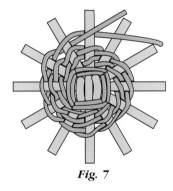

Fig. 7

add extra weavers, tuck the end of the new weaver into the loop formed by the preceding pairing, then tuck the end of the old weaver into the loop formed by the following pairing.

TURNING THE STAKES AND BEGINNING TO WEAVE

If needed, score the stakes before turning. Traditionally for twined baskets, once the stakes are upright, the first few rounds of weaving are accomplished with waling (using three or more weavers). This is a good practice to follow when working with new materials. The waling will help to establish the spacing between upright elements, and adds a sturdy edge to the base that will help prevent the basket from tipping when it is sitting on a flat surface.

Three-Rod Wale

A *three-rod wale* is worked with three separate weavers that are woven in sequence over two stakes and under one, as shown in figures 8 to 11.

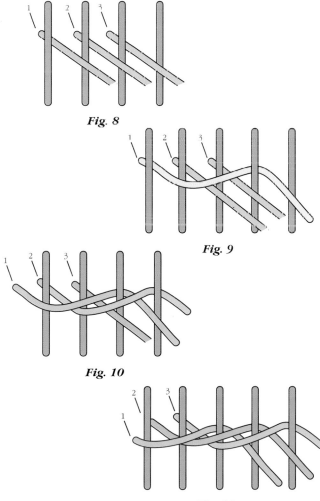

Fig. 8

Fig. 9

Fig. 10

Fig. 11

Four-Rod Wale

A *four-rod wale* is worked with four separate weavers that are woven in sequence either over three stakes and behind one (figure 12), or over two stakes and under two (figure 13).

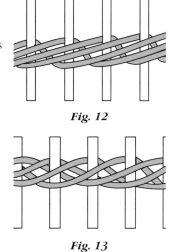

Fig. 12

Fig. 13

Once you've worked a few rows of three-rod or four-rod waling, you can go back to pair twining to complete the basket, or you can combine pairing and waling in any combination to achieve the desired look for the design of your basket. Depending on the material you use, you can add extra twists between stakes when pairing for an added decorative element. This works well (and looks great) with wire.

FINISHES

Traditionally, you finish twined baskets by bending the stakes over, then interweaving them to create a decorative edge. When working with new materials, however, you will most often need to devise a finishing method that suits the material you are using. The description for the track border provided below will help you get started. (Note: There are too many finishes to cover here. The individual projects will provide any specific finishes as needed.)

Track borders are so named because the bent-over stakes track each other around the basket. As shown in figure 14, bend the stakes, then start by taking each in sequence, over two, under one, and over one, until you reach the end of the stake. When you begin, make sure you leave space as indicated to accommodate the last stakes that you will weave. You can vary the pattern of track borders by taking the ends of the stakes under one and over two, or under one and over one.

Fig. 14

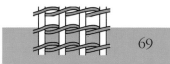

Miniature Wire Basket

Designer Karen Kaushansky made this basket as a project for inter-
mediate weavers. Beginners who have successfully completed two or
three other twining projects in
this book may want to take this
on as a good test of their newfound skills.

Designer: **KAREN KAUSHANSKY**

MATERIALS

Telephone wire, in four colors of your choice

TOOLS

Ruler
Wire cutters
Permanent marker

INSTRUCTIONS

Note: The instructions are for the brown and orange basket shown in the photo at the right.

1 Cut 16 spokes from one color of telephone wire, each approximately 10 inches (25 cm) long. Place one group of four horizontally. Place another group of four vertically over the horizontal group. Arrange the last two groups crosswise on the first two. The arrangement should look like the spokes of a wheel. To help you keep track of your starting point, use the marker to make a mark on the end of one of the spokes that begins a group of four. Even out the ends, and center the crossing point.

2 Take a piece of wire approximately 24 inches (61 cm) long and weave over and under each set of four in a clockwise rotation, until you have gone around all the sets four times.

3 Now turn the base over, and do the same thing going backwards (since you turned the base over, this means you will still work in a clockwise rotation), weaving over the ones that were under the last time and under the ones that were over. As in step 2, do this for four rows.

4 After completing steps 2 and 3, separate the spokes into groups of two and begin a chase

weave. To do this, go all the way around with one weaver, then, when you get back to the starting point, add a second weaver that will go under where you went over with the first weaver (the weavers will chase each other). Keeping the base as flat as possible, continue chase weaving for approximately 2 inches (5 cm).

5 To make the stand at the base of the basket, separate the spokes into singles, and use four weavers to work a four-rod wale (see page 69) in an over three, behind one pattern. When you get to the last three weavers, wale backwards from the last one (furthest on the right) going over three and in, next over three and in, etc., to finish the wale.

6 Choosing colors different than the color of your spokes (either three different color weavers, or two of one color and one of another), begin anywhere on the circle and work a three-rod wale (see page 69) for five rows. Using a weaver the same color as the spokes, do one row of three-rod waling in the same direction.

7 Using the same color combination you used in step 6, begin (where the last row left off) working a three-rod wale in the *opposite* direction, working this way for eight or nine rows. Shape the basket as you go. Using the same color you used for the spokes, work one row of three-rod waling going in the same direction.

8 Working in the same direction as you did in step 6 (opposite from step 8), use the same color combination and work a three-rod wale for five rows, pulling the basket in tighter as you work to shape the neck.

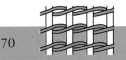

9 At the top, leave approximately 3 to 4 inches (7.5 to 10 cm) of each spoke for the border. For the first row of the border, take one spoke over the next two and out, working this way around the rim. For the second row, take one spoke under the next two and in all the way around.

10 You can stop here and snip off the ends close to the place where they are lying against a spoke. If you want a more finished-looking border on the inside, and you have enough spoke, go over two and under the next one, snipping the ends as close as possible.

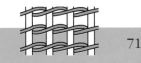

Grapevine Tin

*You can make a basket from most anything!
This project twines grapevine around the rim
of a rustic, galvanized tin
planter, which can be purchased in a craft-supply store.*

Designer: **MOLLY GARDNER**

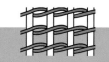

MATERIALS

Tin planter
Grapevine wreath
Silk ivy leaves (optional)

TOOLS

Awl
Small piece of wood, 2 to 3 inches wide (5 to 7.5 cm)
Bucket or tub
Pruning shears
Scissors

INSTRUCTIONS

1 Using the awl, punch holes around the top rim of the container, spacing the holes approximately ¾ inch (1.9 cm) apart. As you punch each hole from the outside of the rim, hold the piece of wood on the inside of the rim. This will guide the awl and keep it from slipping.

2 In the bucket or tub, soak the grapevine wreath in warm water for approximately one hour, or until it is flexible. Using the pruning shears, cut your stakes from the straighter pieces of the vine. Cut one for each hole that you punched, making each 8 inches (20 cm) long.

3 Insert the spokes into the holes, leaving 4-inch (10 cm) ends on the inside of the tin. When all the spokes are in place, make a simple border weave to secure them in place (see figure 1). This is done by starting with any spoke and bringing it over the spoke to the right, then down. Continue all the way around, bringing the last spoke over and down into the place you started.

4 Bend the spokes upward on the outside of the tin. Cut your weavers from the grapevine. Insert two weavers behind two consecutive spokes, then pair twine several rows. End with a basic rolled border. Make the first row of the border by starting with any spoke and bringing it behind the one to the right and out. Continue all the way around. Make the second row of the border by bringing the ends that are out in front, over two spokes, then to the inside of the twining. Trim the spokes to 1 inch (2.5 cm). Don't cut them too short.

5 If desired, use silk ivy leaves to decorate a portion of the planter where the twining meets the tin. You could also use other sprigs of silk leaves or dried flowers, changing the decorations with the season. To keep the tin from rusting when using it as a planter, line the bottom with plastic or polystyrene.

VARIATIONS

Any vine can be twined, coiled, or woven around the rim of the planter. You could also use jute or twine as your weavers for a different look.

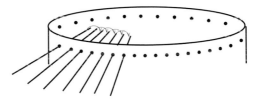

Fig. 1

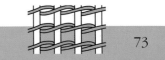

Mini Necklace

If you've never worked in miniature before, challenge yourself with this design, it's easier than it looks! Once you finish, you'll be rewarded with a lovely piece of unique jewelry to keep or give as a gift. Telephone wire provides endless color choices.

Designer: JOANNE WOOD PETERS

MATERIALS

Telephone wire, found in home-supply stores, scrap yards, and through wire suppliers

TOOLS

Scissors or wire cutters
Tweezers

INSTRUCTIONS

Finished dimensions: Base, 1 inch (2.5 cm); height, ⅞ inch (2.2 cm); rim diameter, 1⅛ inches (2.7 cm)

1 Telephone wire is composed of individual wires that are bundled and wrapped in a plastic coating to make one element. To prepare for use, you will need to use scissors or wire cutters to strip the outer wrapping to expose the colored wires. If the telephone wire is for inside work, the wire will be striped; if used for outside lines, it will be a solid color. Once you expose the wire, cut 16 spokes of one color, each 12 inches (30 cm) long.

2 Take eight spokes. Cross four spokes at right angles over four spokes. Using two different colors of wire, twine four rows around the center to lash the cross together. Lay the other eight spokes at right angles over the ones already twined together, then twine two more rows. Separate all the spokes into pairs and twine two more rows.

3 Bring the spokes up to form the sides. Keeping the spokes in pairs, continue twining for eight more rows.

4 Begin making the border at any point on the rim by bringing a first pair of spokes behind the next, or second pair, to the right. Then bring the ends of the first pair out to the front of the basket. Repeat this around the basket.

5 When you are back to the first pair of spokes in step 4, bring that first pair of spokes in front of the second pair to the right. Insert the ends of the first pair between the second pair of spokes and also between the next pair, the third pair, to the right. Bring the ends of the first pair to the inside of the basket. Repeat this sequence around the basket, then trim the ends of the spokes.

6 To make the handle, insert three wires, worked as one, into the rim. Braid the three wires until the handle is as long as desired, making sure the handle fits the proportion of the basket. Trim the ends of the braid if necessary. Then insert the ends of the braid, worked as one, into the other side of the rim.

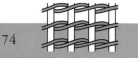

Plant-Fiber Paper Basket

The base and the bottom rows of this basket are twined from seagrass. The seagrass spokes are then sandwiched between two layers of plant-fiber paper to form the majority of the basket's sides. The tops of the spokes can either be twined or fringed. Follow Deb Curtis's recipe for plant-fiber paper on page 77, or use purchased paper pulp which you can buy where paper-making supplies are sold.

Designer: **DEB CURTIS**

MATERIALS

Sea grass, available where basket-making
    supplies are sold
Non-stick cooking spray
Plant-fiber pulp, or purchased paper pulp

TOOLS

Glass jar, straight-sided
Tape measure
Scissors
Clothespins

INSTRUCTIONS

1 Find a straight-sided jar that is the same diameter you want for your basket. The jar should be as tall or taller than the finished basket. To find the length you need for each spoke, measure the jar and use the formula base + height + height (see page 11). Depending on how you will finish the top, add from 4 to 12 inches (10 to 30 cm) to that measurement (you will need more for twining, less for fringe).

2 Cut eight seagrass spokes to the length you determined in step 1. For baskets that are less than 3 inches (7.5 cm) in diameter, use #1 seagrass. For those 3 inches (7.5 cm) and larger, use #2 seagrass. Hold four of the spokes horizontally, and lay the other four spokes on top of these vertically. Use clothespins at each corner to hold the spokes in position.

3 Cut a piece of seagrass for your weaver that is 7 feet (2.1 m) long. Fold this piece unevenly in half, making one tail 4 inches (10 cm) longer than the other one. Pick up the base, remove the clothespins, and place the fold of the weaver around the set of spoke ends that are pointing away from you. Pair twine around the four sets of spokes twice to lash the spokes together. Mark your starting point by tying a piece of string or twist-tie on the starting spoke.

4 Even up all the spoke ends so they are within ¼ inch (.6 cm) of each other in length. Hold the center of the base and pull up both ends of one spoke. Pull the shorter end until both ends are the same length. Use this spoke to measure the other three spokes in that set, adjusting them as necessary. Repeat this with the other sets of four spokes. Be

careful not to pull the spoke all the way out of your center weaving!

5 Separate each set of four spokes into pairs. Twine around each of these sets for two complete rounds. Now separate each spoke into singles, twining around each individual spoke. Weave the base as flat as possible, making its diameter the same diameter of the jar.

6 Once your base is the correct size, hold the spokes up as you twine to form the walls of the basket. Continue twining until you are at the height where you want the paper to begin. Note: If you need to add more seagrass weavers, tuck the short end down, next to a spoke, for two rows. On the other side of the same spoke, tuck in the end of the new weaver and continue twining as if you hadn't stopped.

7 Slip the jar into the seagrass basket you just made. Make sure it fits the way you want it to. Tighten or loosen the twining as necessary. Typically you don't need to leave room for the pulp on the jar (see step 8), since the pulp's thickness is nominal. Pull the jar out and spray it with non-stick cooking spray.

8 Pat the paper pulp onto the greased jar in the area you want the pulp to be on your basket. Use a relatively dry pulp, and overlap the edges of new pulp with pulp already on the jar. Once the jar is covered with pulp, carefully place a towel around it, and roll it in the towel pressing down the whole time and *not sideways*. This helps the pulp to stick together and stay on the jar.

9 Place the pulp-covered jar into the seagrass basket, adjusting the spokes in place. Pat more paper pulp over the spokes, pressing hard to help it adhere to the inside pulp. Once the jar and spokes are covered with pulp, place your nearly complete basket in a towel and roll it again, pressing firmly down. (This helps the two layers of pulp adhere to each other. Let the basket dry. When the paper is completely dry, carefully slip a knife down between the paper and the jar. Often just loosening the top edge will be enough. Slip the jar out, being careful not to rip the paper.

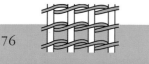

10 Finish the top. You can either continue twining for a few rows, or separate the seagrass spokes by untwisting them to make fringe. To continue twining, take a long weaver and fold it in half unevenly (as in step 3), place it around a spoke, and twine to the desired height. To end the twining, cut the ends of the weavers off. Be sure each end will lay behind a spoke. Generally the ends are behind two adjacent spokes. Another option is to cut each end off long enough to tuck down next to a spoke and under at least two rows of weaving. Finally, fringe your spokes' ends.

Making Plant-Fiber Pulp

Deb Curtis says, "I am truly a basket weaver. Being frugal, I save my basketry scraps to use for handmade paper. I've made great paper from iris leaves, cattails, bamboo sheaths, and cedar bark."

To make the paper

Please note that any utensils and pots used for making paper should not be used for food preparation.

1 Fill an old enamel canner (I find them at yard sales pretty cheap) about half full of plant scraps that have been cut into ½ to 1-inch (1.3 to 2.5 cm) pieces. Fill the canner with water to cover the pieces. You can put an old board on top of the fiber to keep it from floating. Let the water and plant fiber sit at least overnight and up to two days before boiling it. When you are ready to boil it, add 8 tablespoons of soda ash. Stir the mixture with a stick or an old wooden spoon to help dissolve the soda ash.

2 Cover the pot and boil the plant fibers and soda ash for three to four hours. (I do my boiling outside on an old hot plate to keep the fumes out of the house.) After the first two hours, and periodically afterwards, wear heavy rubber gloves to check and see if the plant fiber pulls and slips apart easily when rubbed through your fingers. When the fibers slip apart, rinse them until no more suds wash out and the water runs clear. Note: If using cedar bark, the water will never run clear, since cedar has so much natural dye in it. Once rinsed completely, prepare the fiber to store or blend for use. If you are going to use it right away, skip step 3.

3 (Optional) To store the fiber, dry it in an old onion mesh bag on your clothesline or freeze it. You can store it in the refrigerator for up to four days. If I dry it, I resoak it overnight before blending it. If it's frozen, I thaw it, then pry it apart first before blending.

4 Put a small golf-ball-size chunk of the fiber in a blender with about 3 cups (.72 L) of water. Blend it at the highest speed until the fibers are separated. Blend it for about 20 seconds, turn the blender off, then blend it again for 15 seconds. Put this *slurry* into a plastic colander lined with netting. The water runs out leaving only the plant pulp. Use this pulp to make the body of the basket.

TIP: When using cedar bark, blend it with abaca or cotton linters purchased from a paper supplier. Use about 60 percent cedar bark and 40 percent linters. Linters are just heavy sheets of pure fiber that have already been pulped and are dried as a thick sheet. To use linters, soak a 5-inch-square (12.5 cm) piece in water for a few minutes, then rip that into small ½- to 1-inch (1.3 to 2.5 cm) pieces. Put these in the blender with the plant fiber. Blend all, and pour this mixture into the colander. (I do have plenty of cedar scraps for sale if you would like to try this!)

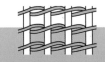

Copper and Brass Wire Basket with Beads

Brass and copper wire, plus crystal-cut beads, make this handsome little basket shine in any part of the house.

Designer: VICKI JOHNSON

After completing the basket, you can spray the wire with clear varnish to prevent it from tarnishing, or you can periodically clean it using a jeweler's cloth.

MATERIALS

18-gauge copper wire
24-gauge copper wire
20-gauge copper wire
22-gauge copper wire
24-gauge brass wire
24, 7mm Czech glass beads

TOOLS

Wire cutters
Permanent marker
Small, smooth-jaw, flat-nose pliers; if your pliers
    have serrated jaws, wrap them in electrical tape
    to prevent them from marring the wire
Round-nose pliers

INSTRUCTIONS

1   Cut 12 lengths of the 18-gauge copper wire, each 18 inches (45 cm) long. Mark the centers of at least two of the wires. Lay six of the wires vertically in front of you. Lay the other six wires horizontally on top the vertical wires, matching the centers, to create four sets of six wires each.

2   Using a length of 24-gauge copper wire, pair twine around the four sets of six wires for three rows to lash them together. Using a permanent marker, mark the tip of your starting spoke. Separate the wires into sets of three, and pair twine around

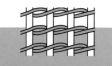

the sets for three rows. Separate the wires into sets of two, and pair twine around the sets for three rows. Then separate the wires into singles and pair twine around them until the base is approximately 2¾ inches (7 cm) in diameter. When you add a new weaver, use the hidden join shown in figure 1. The join will want to pop out if not held; hold it in place with one hand until you have completed a few weaves. End your weavers at the place you started (where you marked the starting spoke). Twist the weavers together to end them.

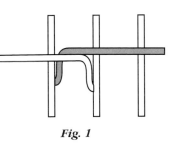

Fig. 1

3   Using the flat-nose pliers, bend the spokes upright as close to the base as possible. Use the 20-gauge copper wire to do one row of four-rod waling (see page 69) in an over three, under one pattern. Start by cutting four pieces of wire, each long enough to go around your basket 1½ times. Start each wire behind a separate spoke with the long end of the wire going out to the right. Work the four-rod wale. When you get back to the beginning, tuck the wires under their first weave. Finish the ends by twisting two wires together. The starting wires should be twisted together inside the basket. The ending wires are twisted together at the base.

4   For the walls of the basket, use the 22-gauge wire to work a three-rod wale (see page 69) in an over two, under one pattern. Start by cutting three lengths 1 to 1½ yards (.9 - 1.4 m) long. The three pieces should all be different lengths to avoid adding three new weavers at the same time. Start the wires behind three separate spokes. After you have woven a few weaves, go back and twist the starting wires together. Add new weavers by twisting a new wire onto the old wire with the pliers. Work the three-rod wale for 11 to 12 rows. End where you started to keep the basket level. Twist all three wires together for a neat, clean finish. Be careful not to twist the wires too tightly; they will pull the spokes, moving them out of place and distorting the basket.

5   Use the 24-gauge brass wire to work a three-rod wale for three rows. Twist the wires together at the start and again when you finish your three rows. End where you started to kept the basket level. Add 12 beads, placing one on every other spoke. Simply slide the bead onto the spoke and place it on top of the brass wire. Then use the 24-gauge brass wire to work a three-rod wale for two rows, twisting the ends together at the start and finish. Add 12 more beads to every other spoke; they should alternate from the first row of beads. Use 24-gauge brass wire to work a three-rod wale for three rows, twisting the wires together at the start and finish.

6   Use the 22-gauge copper wire to work a three-rod wale for eight rows, twisting the ends of the wires together at the start and finish. Pack the rows down with your fingers. There should be no gaps between your rows. Bend all the spokes of your basket down at 90° angles. Cut all the spokes to a length of 4 inches (10 cm). Then coil the ends around your round-nose pliers. Note: You will form the coil with the round-nose pliers, but will have to finish with the flat-nose pliers and your fingers. Once all the spokes have been coiled, turn every other one down vertically to complete your basket.

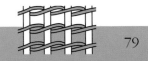

Mini Burden Basket

Early Native Americans used large baskets to carry their food, wood, and belongings—they called them burden baskets. Make your own mini version from materials you probably have on hand. Weaving materials can be twine, jute, yarn, threads, cord, leather strips, and vines. You can also mix in natural materials from the garden, such as iris and lily leaves and other vines.

Designer: **MOLLY GARDNER**

MATERIALS

Smooth vine, such as nito vine, which comes
    wrapped as a wreath and can be found in most
    craft-supply stores
Twine, hemp, jute, or waxed linen thread
Assorted materials for weaving
Embellishments, such as beads, feathers, and charms

TOOLS

Pruning shears
Darning needle

INSTRUCTIONS

1 Find smooth, straight portions of the vine. From them, cut eight spokes, each 22 inches (56 cm) long. Mark the center point of each spoke.

2 To make the base, first cut a 2-yard (1.8 m) piece of twine, hemp, jute, or waxed linen thread for your weaver. Take four spokes and lay them vertically side by side. Take the other four spokes and place them horizontally over the vertical spokes. Adjust the spokes so they cross at their center points. Take the weaver and fold in half. Fold it over the first set of spokes and pair twine around each set of spokes for three rows to lash the spokes together. It helps to mark the first spoke with a twist tie or black marker then you can easily count the rows.

3 Begin shaping the spokes into a cone shape. You will be weaving with the spokes facing away from you. Separate the 16 spokes into eight pairs, and twine for three rows. Then separate the spokes into individual spokes, twining them individually for the remainder of the basket. Keep shaping the basket into a cone by pushing sharply down on the spokes as you twine.

4 If you run out of weaver, simply lay in a new piece and continue twining. Once the base is shaped, you will want to change to a different color or type of material. Continue twining with any materials you like. Use your imagination and have fun!

5 When you have approximately 5 inches (12.5 cm) of spoke left, it is time to make your border or rim. Invert the basket, placing only the ends of the spokes in warm water for one minute, or until flexible. Be careful to avoid getting the twined rows wet.

6 There are many border variations, and you can make any border you desire. A basic, easy border is the rolled border. To make it, begin the first row by taking one spoke behind the one to its right, then out to the outside. Repeat this all the way around the rim, tucking the last spoke under the first one. For row two, take one spoke, which is now in front, over two spokes to its right, then to the inside of the twining. Trim the ends evenly. Don't cut them too short or they will come out.

7 Using a darning needle, thread strands of waxed thread through the basket and tie with a square knot. String on some beads for decoration. To make a hanging feather, put a drop of craft glue on the end of the feather and insert it into a bead. Make a hanger by cutting a length of twine approximately 12 inches (30 cm) long and tying it onto the rim.

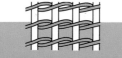

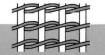

Twig Cans

Use these as mini-sculptures when making a display of beach mementos—a bit of sand, a few shells, beach glass, a gull feather. . . However, if you really _must_ have them _do_ something, use them as

Designer: **DYAN MAI PETERSON**

planters for miniature ivies or other small climbing- plant varieties.

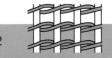

MATERIALS

Assortment of twigs with bark still on
Two 15-ounce (425 g) food cans
Matte-finish spray paint in black
Spray-on metal primer (optional)
Hemp twine
1.75 mm round reed, 3 yards (2.75 m)
Assorted shells and beads

TOOLS

Pruning shears
Wide rubber bands
Scissors

INSTRUCTIONS

1 Gather or glean the twigs. You may want to have many more on hand than you think you need; that way you can match the twigs for uniformity of thickness as you work. Cut the twigs to a pleasing length. I like the wild look of longer twigs randomly going here and there. You may prefer a tamer look, and will need to cut your twigs accordingly.

2 Remove the labels from two 15-ounce (425 g) food cans. Make sure the cans are clean and dry. Apply the spray paint inside and out. Two or three light coats work better than one heavy one. If you are planning on using the cans outdoors, you may want to spray the cans with metal primer before applying the paint.

3 One can was made using round reed, the other using hemp twine. If you are working with reed, soak it in water for approximately two hours before use to make it pliable.

4 Lay the twigs next to each other, laying out approximately the number you will need to circle each can. Place two rubber bands on each can, one toward the top, the other toward the bottom. You may need to search for just the right bands. They should be fairly wide and fit snugly to the can without having to double them.

5 Begin inserting the twigs next to the can, with the rubber bands holding them in place. Completely encircle the can with twigs.

6 Take a length of reed or twine, fold it in half and begin pair twining around the twigs. Twine as tightly as possible. The can with reed has two rows of twining separated by approximately 2 inches (5 cm). The can with hemp has three, two-row sets of twining separated by approximately ½ inch (1.3 cm). When you've completed a row, or set of rows, you may need to slide the rubber band(s) out of your way; do so as needed. When you have completed twining, cut the rubber bands off; do not attempt to slide them off.

7 Embellish the cans as desired. The can with hemp has short lengths of hemp tied randomly on the twigs. The can with reed is decorated with shells strung on a piece of twine that is tied to a twig.

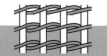

Sisal and Copper Wire Basket

Pairing the smooth metallic finish of copper wire with the rough texture of sisal roping makes for an interesting juxtaposition of materials. Allow the wire to age, and you will have a basket that changes its look over time.

Designer: **Jane LaFerla**

MATERIALS

1/4-inch (.6 cm) sisal rope
Masking tape
16-gauge copper wire, approximately 50 feet (15 m)
18-gauge copper wire, approximately 150 feet (45 m)

TOOLS

Tin snips
Pencil
Awl
Wire cutters
Needle-nose pliers

INSTRUCTIONS

Finished dimensions: Base, 5½ inches (13.8 cm) in diameter; height, 4½ inches (11.3 cm)

1 Using the tin snips, cut eight lengths of sisal rope, each 28 inches (71 cm) long. With a pencil, mark the center point of each length. If you purchased sisal rope packaged in a coil, the rope will retain a circular shape after cutting. It is easier to manipulate the rope if you let it relax, allowing it to lose some of its curl. You may find it helpful to extend the lengths, then tape their ends to a flat surface for a few hours before you begin working.

2 Since a double thickness of rope will cause the bottom of the basket to rock, you will insert the spokes into each other to make your base as flat as possible. Begin by taking one length of rope and untwisting it close to the center point marked by the pencil. Note that this separates the two-ply twist into two smaller pieces of rope. Take another length, do not untwist it, and insert it between the two smaller pieces. You may find it helpful to use an awl to help keep the plies separated while inserting this length. Using the pencil marks as your guide, center the two lengths so they cross at their middle points. Next, insert three more untwisted lengths next to this one. You will need to keep untwisting the first length of rope to accommodate each length you insert. When they are all inserted, center the four lengths of rope, using their middle points as a guide. The inserted lengths will be the vertical spokes.

3 Take another piece of rope, and untwist it at its middle point. Untwist enough to accommodate the width of the four pieces of rope. Thread it onto the four vertical spokes. Repeat, using the last two lengths of rope. Adjust the horizontal and vertical spokes, making sure their ends are equal. You will now have four groups of four spokes crossing at a center point.

4 Using the wire cutters, cut a 36-inch (.9 m) length of 18-gauge wire. Fold the length in half. Place the fold around one group of four spokes, then pair twine around each group three times to lash them together. Try to make the twining as tight and even as possible.

5 After the third row of twining, separate the individual spokes by pair twining around each spoke. Mark your starting point by twisting a small length of wire to the end of the first spoke. As you twine, try to make the distance between the spokes as even as possible. If you run out of wire, cut lengths as needed. Try to leave ends that are approximately 1½ inches (3.8 cm) long. Do not be concerned about working the ends into the twining at this point; you will be able to hide them and cut them once the basket is complete. Continue twining until the diameter of the base is approximately 5 inches (12.5 cm).

6 Make the rim of your base. Cut three lengths of 16-gauge wire, each approximately 30 inches (76 cm) long. Insert each end into the spaces between three successive spokes. Work a three-rod wale (over two, under one) for four rows. Add new weavers as necessary.

7 Cut two lengths of 18-gauge wire. Insert both ends into one space between two spokes. Place one wire over the next spoke and one under. Twine the sides, making this one variation as you work: Instead of crossing the wire weavers once between spokes, give them an extra twist, crossing the wires

twice. This will help separate the spokes, and make the sides of the basket stronger. The first few rows will shape the basket. Use a little extra tension when working them to help move the spokes into an upright position. Do not apply too much tension, or you will draw the sides in, distorting the shape of the basket. Continue twining (with a twist), adding new weavers as necessary, until the twining reaches a height of 3 inches (7.5 cm).

8 End the twining at the first spoke, the one you marked in step 5. Work all the wire ends to the inside of the basket. Using the needle-nose pliers, work the ends into the adjoining twining for approximately 1 inch (2.5 cm). Use the wire cutters to cut any ends.

9 Make the border. Starting with the first and second spokes, take the right-hand spoke and loop it under the left-hand spoke. Encircle the left spoke, then tuck the end of the right spoke into its own loop. Continue in this way around the border. When all spokes are looped, go around the border pulling the ends to secure them and even them out. To wrap the end, cut one 10-inch (25 cm) length of wire for each spoke. Approximately 1 inch (2.5 cm) in from the end of the spoke, lay one end of the wire next to the rope. Wrap the wire around the end (to hide it) while you are wrapping the rope with the wire. Leave a ¼-inch (.6 cm) tail. Use the needle-nose pliers to tuck the ends of the wire into the wrapping. Fray the ends of the rope by separating the individual fibers.

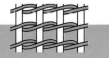

Sea Urchins

The rounded shape and rimless bottom of these miniature double-wall baskets provide a smooth organic look, reminding

Designer: **LYNN B. GAMMON**

designer Lynn Gammon of colorful sea urchins. While this project is suitable for all weaving levels, some previous experience with twining is helpful.

MATERIALS

50 strands of Mizuhiki cords, each 36 inches (.9 m) in length:
30 in color A; 10 in color B; and 10 in color C

TOOLS

Scissors
Needle-nose pliers

INSTRUCTIONS

Finished dimensions: Approximately 2 to 3 inches (5 to 7.5 cm) high by 4 to 5 inches (10 to 12.5 cm) wide.

Note: You will weave the inside basket first, then the outside basket.

INSIDE BASKET

use only color A

1 Take one strand and fold it, making one side 14 inches (35 cm) long and the other side 22 inches (56 cm) long. When you fold it, make sure to crease firmly to hold the fold. Set aside. This will be your first weaver.

2 Take four strands and cut them in half, giving you eight spokes, each 18 inches (45 cm) long. Pick up four spokes and hold them in your hand so they are vertical. Place the remaining four spokes horizontally across the four vertical spokes.

3 Take the folded strand from step 1, and place it around the top four vertical spokes. Using the two ends as weavers, pair twine around the crossing point of the spokes. After you have woven around the center twice, stop to even up the length of the spokes.

(Because the material is smooth, it is much easier to do this at this stage.) When the spokes are even, cut out one spoke to the base, leaving you with 15 spokes. Mark your starter spoke. The easiest way to do this with this material is to bend the end of the starter spoke over ¼ inch (.6 cm).

4 Split the spokes into eight groups, making seven pairs of two spokes and one single spoke. Pair twine around those twice. Next, divide the groups into individual spokes, and weave around the 15 spokes two more times. Add an additional weaver and begin three-rod waling (see page 69). Note that for the inside of the basket, you will be doing a *reverse* three-rod waling to allow the smoother side of the weaving to appear on the inside. To do this, pass each weaver *under* two spokes and *over* the third spoke (rather than the usual over two spokes and under the third).

5 Continue weaving this pattern until you reach the top of the basket, shaping the basket as you weave. If you need to add new weavers, don't worry about hiding the ends, they will be hidden between the walls. Keep the inside of the basket facing away from you as you work; it is easier to shape the basket this way. I normally weave 20 rows in an outward direction before starting to curve the basket inward. After I turn the basket to the upper rim, I add approximately 14 more rows of weaving. The numbers may vary according to the way you weave.

6 When the top opening of the basket is approximately 1 inch (2.5 cm) in diameter, it is time to weave the rim. Begin by cutting off two of the weavers, leaving tails that are approximately ½ inch

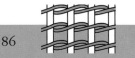

(1.3 cm) long. (You will eventually tuck them under the outer wall.) As you work, be careful to avoid inserting the remaining weaver into the rim. Next, take any one of the spokes and pass it to the right, placing it behind the spoke on its right, then bring it back to the outside. This first spoke will now be positioned between the second and third spoke to its right. Now take the second spoke and pass it behind the third spoke and then to the outside. Continue this pattern until you have woven all the spokes in the same manner. Weave the last spoke by gently lifting up the first spoke, then passing the last spoke in the same manner as the rest of the rim. After completing the first weaving pass around the rim, the spokes should extend out rather than up. Gently tug on the spokes to tighten them up.

7 The second and third weaving passes on the rim are similar to the first, except you will be passing over two spokes each time. Since the spokes are not facing outward, I find it easier to weave these next two rows while holding the basket in my right hand, placing the woven spokes under my hand as I weave. When you complete the third row, again, tug on the spokes to tighten them. Then, hold the rim firmly (to prevent unraveling) and pull down on the spokes to realign them in a vertical position. This will ease the weaving of the outside of the basket.

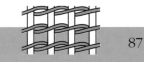

OUTSIDE BASKET
use all three colors

8 The remaining weaver from the inside of the basket (the one you didn't cut in step 6 will be naturally aligned in the opposite direction from which you will now be weaving. Reverse its direction by turning it and crimping (bending) the cord to stay in the new position. In the two spaces to the right of this weaver, insert two additional weavers, one each in colors B and C. Use these three weavers to weave a three-rod wale. Unlike the inside of the basket, weave the three-rod wale in the usual manner (not in reverse), bringing each weaver over two spokes and under the third. Continue to weave this pattern until you reach the bottom of the basket.

9 Continue weaving down the sides and across the base of the inner basket until the opening is as small as you can weave it. Then, cut the weavers, leaving each with a ½-inch (1.3 cm) tail. Tuck the tails up into the inside of the basket between the two walls. Cut the spokes to make them even, leaving tails approximately ½ inch (1.3 cm) long. Following figure 1, cross the tails over each other, and insert the ends between the two walls of the basket. Since you will be inserting the last spokes under the beginning spokes, use the needle-nose pliers to lift the beginning spokes to ease the insertion of the last spokes. Once all the spokes are inserted, gently press the spokes down for a smoother finish.

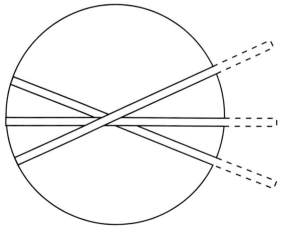

Fig. 1

Basket Ball

While you're at it. . . This variation of the same technique, worked around a polystyrene ball, is a natural for making distinctive holiday ornaments or year-round hanging decorations.

TO MAKE THE BASKET BALL YOU WILL NEED:

20 strands of Mizuhiki cords, each 36 inches (.9 m) in length: 8 in color A; 6 in color B; and 6 in color C
2-inch (5 cm) polystyrene ball
1 small jump ring
1, ⅜-inch (.9 cm) or ½-inch (1.3 cm) diameter pronged stud (you can use either size)
1 round-head pin

INSTRUCTIONS

1 Begin by following step 1 from Sea Urchins, using a strand of color A. Taking two strands of color A, cut them in half, then in half again, giving you eight spokes, each 9 inches (22.5 cm) long. Slip the jump ring over one bundle of four spokes.

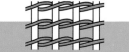

2 Pick up the four spokes without the jump ring, and hold them in your hand so they are vertical. Place the four spokes with the jump ring horizontally across the four vertical spokes. Center the jump ring on the vertical spokes.

3 Follow step 3 for Sea Urchins. However, *do not cut out one spoke.* You will need 16 spokes for this project.

4 Split the four groups of four spokes into eight groups of two spokes, and pair twine around those twice. Next, pair twine around the 16 individual spokes two more times. Place the weaving on the polystyrene ball, securing it to the ball with a round-head pin placed between the spokes at the center of the weaving.

5 Cut off one end of one of the weavers, leaving a ½-inch (1.3 cm) end. Tuck this end in by sticking it directly into the ball. There will now be one strand of color A coming from between two spokes. At the next opening between spokes, stick one end of a color B strand into the ball. Then, at the next opening, stick one end of a color C strand in. You should now have three weavers, one each in color A, B, and C. Begin three-rod waling. Note: Whenever you run out of a weaver, stick the end directly into the ball, then replace it by sticking one end of the new weaver into the ball at the same spot.

6 Continue the three-rod waling. Before you reach the bottom of the ball, while there is still room, insert the pronged stud into the center bottom of the ball. This will give the ball a nicely finished look. Continue weaving until you can no longer fit the weavers between the spokes; then cut the weavers, leaving each with a ½-inch (1.3 cm) tail. Tuck the tails up into the foam ball under the weaving.

7 Cut the spokes to make them even, leaving tails approximately ½ inch (1.3 cm) long. Cross the tails over the pronged stud at an angle as in figure 1 for Sea Urchins. (The stud will show slightly when finished.) Then insert the spokes as in step 9 for Sea Urchins, to finish.

VARIATIONS

■ For a 2½-inch (6.25 cm) ball, cut eight spokes, each 10 inches (25 cm) long. You will need a total of 27 cords: 11 of color A, 8 of color B, 8 of color C.

■ For a 3-inch (7.5 cm) ball, cut eight spokes, each 11 inches (27.5 cm) long. You will need a total of 34 cords: 14 of color A, 10 of color B, 10 of color C.

TIP: If you are making the Sea Urchins in a different size, or using a different size ball for the Basket Ball, you may end up with a different number of spokes. The following patterns will *always* result as long as you are doing a continuous weave with three weavers. (Consider it a math "thing.")

If the number of spokes, no matter how many, is divisible by three with no remainder, e.g. $15 \div 3 = 5$, you will *always* end up with a stripe/bar pattern.

If the number of spokes is divisible by three with a remainder of one, e.g. $16 \div 3 = 5$ r1, you will *always* end up with a shallow spiral pattern.

If the number of spokes is divisible by three with a remainder of two, e.g. $14 \div 3 = 4$ r2, you will *always* end up with a deep spiral pattern.

About Mizuhiki

Notes from Lynn

The advantages to using Mizuhiki are tremendous. As a tool for color and composition exploration, it is endlessly exciting. The shimmering surface provides extra dimensions to the colors. Even after nine years, I have yet to tire of it.

Mizuhiki is made by gluing Mylar onto a pressed paper cord. The material is very slippery, providing basket makers with a good challenge. If you handle it too roughly, it starts to unravel. My advice is to never use it for projects that require sharp turns, such as rib-construction baskets. I have found that a simple bowl shape works best, but I encourage you to experiment with shapes.

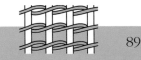

Silver Linings

Start with a gourd...then use your imagination to create your own masterpiece. Designer Linda Sura created a double-weave basket with a gourd interior and a twined-reed exterior. She coated the inside of the gourd with silvery paper pulp for a starry interior.

Designer: LINDA ARTER SURA

MATERIALS

One medium gourd, approximately 6 to 10 inches (15 to 25 cm) in diameter

#2 to #5 round reed (dyed or natural) for spokes; here dyed black

Leather dye in a color of your choice; used here, navy blue

#1 to #3 round reed (dyed or natural) for weavers

20-gauge silver wire

Decorative fibers, such as seagrass, yarn, twine

Waxed linen thread

Paper pulp or papier-mâché; used here, colored pulp Wild Fiber in silver, or select a color of your choice

Embellishments, such as beads and feathers

TOOLS

Small saw, or craft tool with saw attachment

Grapefruit spoon

Pruning shears

Drill and small drill bit, or craft tool with small drill bit

Clothespins

Scissors

Needle

INSTRUCTIONS

1 Plan your color combination by coordinating the colors you will use for the reed, leather dye, and paper interior. Also look for embellishments that will go with your color scheme. Dye reed accordingly.

2 Evenly cut off the top of the gourd. You want to make a large opening so the inside of the finished gourd can be seen. Avoid any sharp curves when cutting the top, since it will be harder to shape. Using a grapefruit spoon, clean the inside of the gourd, scraping all the loose seeds and fiber. Do this in a well-ventilated area; try not to breathe the dust. It is a good idea to wear a dust mask while doing this. If you will be applying paper pulp or papier-mÉchÇ to the inside, it is not necessary to clean it as smoothly as you would if you are going to dye or stain the inside.

3 Using the leather dye in a color of your choice, dye the outside of the gourd and the rim. This gourd is dyed navy blue. It may take several coats to get an even layer of color, so allow the dye to dry a few minutes between coats. You can use a hair dryer to speed up the process. If you are not going to apply pulp or papier-mâché to the inside of the gourd (see step 12), dye or paint the inside.

4 Cut eight spokes of the #5 reed to the following measurement: Measure the gourd from the top of one side around the gourd to the opposite side; add 15 inches (37.5 cm) to allow for the border or other finish. Next take the same measurement, divide it in half, and subtract 4 inches (10 cm). Cut 16 spokes of the #5 reed to this new measurement.

5 Soak the eight spokes cut in step 4 and a long piece of #2 round reed until flexible. Place four of the spokes horizontally, then place the other four vertically across the horizontal ones, centering them where they cross. Take the long piece of #2 round reed, fold it nearly in half, and start pair twining around the four sets of four spokes. Do this for approximately two or three rounds to lash them together. Try to weave as tightly as you can without bunching up the spokes. Mark your starting point by placing a piece of yarn or twist-tie on the first spoke of the first set of four.

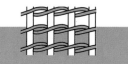

6 Divide the spokes into sets of two spokes each, and twine around each set of two for three rows. Now start twining around individual spokes; do this until the base is nearly the same size as the bottom of the gourd. You should be ready to start up the curve of the gourd. End the twining and tuck in ends.

7 Start to shape the weaving to the gourd by placing the gourd on the base, then continuing to work around the gourd. Using three long pieces of #2 reed, work a three-rod wale for approximately two, or more, rows. (The number of rows worked will depend on the size of the gourd.) Take the shorter spokes cut in step 4 and trim the end of each spoke at an angle, cutting in from the end approximately ½ inch (1.3 cm).

Place the angled ends beside each spoke, and push in for approximately 1 inch (2.5 cm). Continue working a three-rod wale around all the spokes for approximately two to eight rows. As you do, start to curve the spokes at this point. I like to work the three-rod wale until the spokes easily go in an upward direction.

8 Take the sides as started, and pull some of the rows apart at approximately two or three points around the sides. You want to create space (hills and valleys) between the rows; you will eventually work tapestry techniques in the spaces. Then take the 20-gauge silver wire and work a three-rod wale for two rows. To start the wire, I bend an end of the wire, then tuck the bent end in beside a spoke.

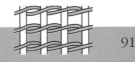

91

9 Take the decorative fiber, such as yarn, #1 or #2 round reed, seagrass, or decorative threads, and pair twine or work a three-rod wale between the spaces created in step 8. To get the tapestry effect, vary your materials or combine them, such as round reed with decorative threads. To make hills, twine over X number of spokes (could be six, seven, or eight, you decide) and then go back. Decrease one spoke each row, as shown in figure 1. To make valleys, do the opposite, as shown in figure 2; start out twining around one or two spokes and then increase a spoke on each side. After you have worked the tapestry techniques, work two more rows of a three-rod wale with the 20-gauge wire.

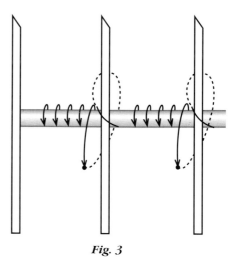

Fig. 3

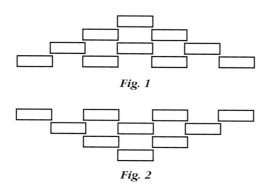

Fig. 1

Fig. 2

10 Continue in this way, alternating the tapestry techniques and a three-rod wale in the wire, until you are approximately 1½ to 2 inches (3.8 to 5 cm) from the top of the gourd. (The silver acts as a dividing line between colors and the hills and valleys.) If you want to add beads in a gap rather than working the tapestry techniques, slip the beads onto the spokes to fill in the gap, then continue as before. To bring it all together, finish the top with three-rod waling in round reed that is the same color as the base. Trim the spokes at an angle approximately 2 to 3 inches (5 to 7.5 cm) from the top of the gourd.

11 Make the rim. With the drill and very small drill bit (to accommodate the linen thread), drill a hole for each spoke, placing the hole very close to the spoke and approximately 1 inch (2.5 cm) from the top of the gourd. Take a piece of #5 reed, and place it around the rim of the gourd, inside the spokes. Use clothespins to clip it to the rim of the gourd. Following figure 3, wrap the waxed linen around the #5 round reed, through the hole, and

around the spoke. Depending on the space between spokes, you may need to wrap the reed several times. (For decorative purposes, I prefer to cover most of the reed with wrapping.)

12 Mix the pulp or papier-mâché according to package directions, and apply to the inside of the gourd. It is easy to do with your hands (or wearing rubber gloves). Try to make it fairly smooth. Allow the pulp or papier-mâché to dry thoroughly; depending on the weather, this may take as long as a day or two. You can speed up the process by using a fan or hair dryer. While it is drying, move the gourd around to prevent the pulp or papier-mâché from mildewing. If the pulp is not colored, or if you are using papier-mâché, paint the inside of the gourd. Then paint the tips of the spokes the same color as the inside color.

VARIATIONS:

■ Use different colors of reed, dye, beads, and wire. Use several colors of leather dye for the outside of the gourd, letting the colors bleed together.

■ Use different sizes of reed. If you have a bigger gourd, you may want to start out with #4 or #5 round reed, then weave with #2 or #3. Try different borders.

■ Add beads at different places, or don't use any beads. Add feathers.

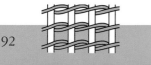

Coiling Basics

YOU CAN IMMEDIATELY identify a coiled basket by its spiraling shape made by stitching together a round *core* element. As shown in figure 1, coiling is more similar to sewing then weaving. As you shape the core material into a spiral, you use a thinner more pliable material (the "thread") to sew each new row of coiling to the previous row. The central core can be composed of a single element, or can be made of thinner elements grouped together to create one thicker core.

Fig. 1

You can use a simple overhand stitch, also called a whipstitch, when coiling. There are also several decorative stitches traditionally associated with this technique. You can place the stitches close together to completely cover the core, or you can space the stitches so the core is visible. You can also wrap the coils while stitching them together using a figure-eight stitch.

The spiral shaping in this technique creates round or oval baskets. When using new materials, any flexible, round element can be used for the core such as plastic tubing, rolled paper, cording, braiding, long leaves, pine needles, or fabrics. Round items that you can string together, such as beads, will also create an effective and dramatic core. The pliable thread element can range from sinew to waxed-linen thread to wire.

MEASURING

There is no formula for calculating the amount of core material needed for your basket. You can make an educated estimate of length based on the finished size of the basket and the diameter of the material you are using for the coil. Experience with the technique will help you make more accurate estimates each time. Be assured, whether you are using one solid element, or grouping thinner elements into one thicker core, adding on additional lengths of core as needed is an easy process.

SHAPING THE SPIRAL

To start the coil, you will need to wrap the end of your core material with your thread element. There are two methods for beginning the wrapping. One way, which is more suitable when using a single-core element, is to simply lay the tail of the thread against the core material; you want to place the tail extending away from the end of the core. Then with the remaining length of thread, begin wrapping the core from its end, wrapping the tail and core as one, as shown in figure 2.

Fig. 2

The other method is more suitable when grouping elements to create one core. First, gather the elements to create one round core. Next, pass the needle and thread through the ends of the core to secure the thread and bury it in the core. Then wrap the core, positioning the thread as you wrap to completely cover the core. For both methods, continue wrapping until the length of the wrapped end is long enough to curl over itself as you begin shaping the spiral. Do not cut the thread.

Fold the end of the core into itself as shown in figure 3. Keep in mind that the shape of this fold will affect the rest of the basket. If you want to make a round basket, try to keep the fold as tight and round as possible. If you

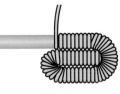

Fig. 3

are making an oval basket, shape the fold into a small oval. If you are making an elongated oval basket, extend the fold into a long oval.

STITCHING THE COILS

When you have the desired shape of your fold, attach the outer coil of the fold to the center element. You can do this by looping the thread around the outer coil and the center element to lash them together, or you can stitch them together using a simple overhand stitch as shown in figure 4. For the stitch, pass the needle and thread through the upper third of the center element. Space the stitches evenly as you work around the fold, placing them approximately ⅛ to ¼ inch (.3 to .6 cm) apart.

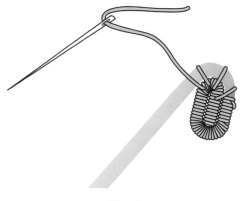

Fig. 4

Once you've secured the fold, you are ready to begin stitching and coiling. If you are making a basket with a visible core, place each stitch to the outside of the stitch in the preceding coil, as shown in figure 5, passing the needle and thread through the upper third of the coil. When working with a visible core, the stitches will get farther and farther apart as the spiral enlarges. When you notice this happening, simply take an extra stitch in between the regular stitching to even

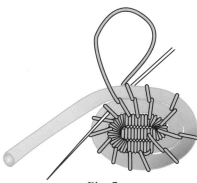

Fig. 5

Fig. 6

out the spacing, as shown in figure 6. Depending on the size of your basket, you may need to add more stitches in between as necessary.

If you are making a basket with a covered core, you can simply place the stitches next to each other, taking each new stitch on the outside of the preceding stitch. You can also wrap and secure the coils at the same time using a figure-eight stitch. Depending on the project you are making and the material you are using, you will wrap the core several times, then make a figure-eight stitch, as shown in figure 7, around the previous coil.

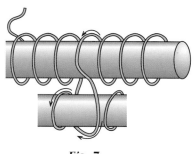

Fig. 7

Adding Thread

When you are running out of thread, plan ahead to leave approximately 3 inches (7.5 cm) for the old tail. Pull the tail out of the coil—do not cut the tail. Thread the needle with the new length of thread. Insert the needle close to the exiting point of the old tail. Pull the needle and thread through the coil, leaving approximately 3 inches (7.5 cm) for the new tail. Using a double knot, tie the old and new tail together, then lay the tied ends together on the core material; as you continue to coil, the tail will be hidden in the core material. If the core material is soft, you can also bury the old and new tails in the core.

Adding Core Material

If you run out of core material, you can easily add some more. If you are working with a single-element core, overlap the ends of the old and new core, then continue coiling and stitching as before. If the core material is thick, you may need to trim the ends to reduce the bulk.

When you are working with thinner elements grouped to make a single core, insert new elements as needed into the bundle of old elements. Note: When working with many elements to make one core, you may need help to ensure a uniform circumference, and to keep the elements together. You can purchase gauges for this purpose from suppliers of basket-making materials, or you can fashion your own by using a ring, or making a ring from wire or metal.

SHAPING THE SIDES

When the coil's measurement reaches the determined diameter for the base of your basket, you are ready to shape the sides. If your basket has straight sides, place the next coil directly on top of the coil preceding it, and continue to coil and stitch as before until the basket is as tall as you desire. To make rounded or flared sides, place each new coil slightly to the outside of the coil preceding it; this will create an increase. Once you have reached the desired increase, you may need to decrease to draw the sides inward. To decrease, place each new coil slightly to the inside of the coil preceding it.

FINISHING

You want to stop your last coil in the same place you started coiling. When the basket is as large as desired, taper the end of the last coil until it gradually blends into the top coil of the preceding round. Work a few overhand (whip) stitches over the end of the core material. Using the needle and thread, work backward to cross-stitch over the previous row of stitching, as shown in figure 8. When you reach the end of the tapered coil, take a few small whipstitches into the coil to secure the end of the thread, then run the needle and thread through the core material for a few inches. Bring the needle and thread out, and cut the end close to the coil.

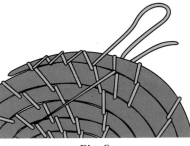
Fig. 8

DECORATIVE STITCHES

You can alter the look of your design by using decorative stitches when working with a visible core. The two most common are explained here. As you become more experienced, you may want to experiment to create your own variations on these stitches.

Split Stitch

This works well when your thread element is a wide material. Stitch around the shaped core, then complete two rows of coiling using the basic overhand

stitch described above. As you start the third coil, bring the needle and thread through the middle of the next stitch in the preceding coil, rather than placing it on the outside of the stitch. (See figure 9.)

Fig. 9

V-Shaped Stitch

This variation of the split stitch can be used with any width of thread element. Work the core and two rows of coiling in the basic overhand stitch, as for the split stitch. As you start the third coil, bring the needle and thread through the middle of the next

Fig. 10

stitch in the preceding coil, rather than placing it on the outside of the stitch. Then take another stitch through that same split stitch. As you continue to coil, take two stitches in each V-shaped space formed by the preceding two stitches. (See figure 10.)

Corrugated Coils with Ribbon Wrap

The wrapped cardboard coils of this basket create a modern version of

Designer: LINDA RAGSDALE

an old technique. This chameleon-type basket is easy to assemble. When seasons change along with the colors, simply unwrap the ribbon and start all over again!

MATERIALS

Large sheets of drawing paper

3 sheets of cardboard, each 24 x 25 inches (61 x 64 cm); you want the corrugated stripes to run vertically on the 24-inch (61 cm) side

Wood glue

16 yards (15 m) of wire-edged ribbon for wrapping; used here, 7/8-inch (2.2 cm) ribbon in black with gold trim

6 yards (5.5 m) of ribbon for decorative trim; used here, 7/8-inch (2.2 cm) ribbon in black with an interwoven flower pattern

4½ yards (4 m) of 7/8-inch (2.2 cm) gold mesh ribbon for trim

1 can of gold spray paint

1 small bottle of gold acrylic paint

Spray sealer

TOOLS

Utility knife with very sharp blade

Scissors

Push pins

INSTRUCTIONS

1 Each piece of the basket is constructed from three layers of cardboard. The pieces are cut separately from each sheet, then glued together. Figure 1 shows the layout pattern you will follow for each piece of cardboard. Note that the pattern allows for an extra set of rings.

2 Following figure 2, make a pattern for your rings. On a separate sheet of paper, measure a center oval to be 2½ inches (6.25 cm) wide and 4 inches (10 cm) long. From the outer edge of this

oval, draw five more ovals, each 1 inch (2.5 cm) wide. There are six ovals all together. Following the layout in figure 1, transfer the ring pattern to each sheet of cardboard.

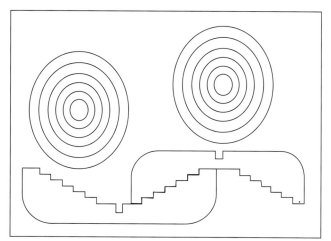

Fig. 1

2 1/2"
(6.25 cm)

4" (10 cm)

Fig. 2

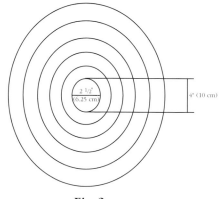

3 Make a pattern for your base on a separate sheet of paper. The base is constructed of one long and one short base that will be locked together in a cross-hair pattern. Note the measurements on the pattern in figure 3. The steps should be 1 inch (2.5 cm) long, with a width that is equivalent to the stacked height of three layers of board; in this case, it is ⅝ inch (1.6 cm). Draw the bases following figure 3; then following the layout in figure 1, transfer the pattern to each sheet of cardboard.

4 Cut out each sheet of cardboard separately, then piece them together. Be careful not to crush the corrugation to maintain the cardboard's strength. When cutting the ovals, position the cardboard to drop off the edge of the table, then pull the blade up and down through the board in a sawing motion. Be sure to hold the blade upright and not at an angle, since this will affect alignment of the edges. Use wood glue to attach each layer. Do not use heavy materials to weight the board while allowing the glue to dry.

5 To assemble the pieces, lock the bases together by aligning the center slots (see figure 2). Place the rings in the base, on the steps, one at a time, from the smallest to largest.

6 Wrap the rings. First, keeping the rings intact as one large oval, mark a small X on the underside of each ring; place each X in alignment with the previous one, giving you a straight line of Xs. This will be the starting point for your wrapping.

7 Punch out the small center oval and set aside. Separate the rings; you will be wrapping one ring at a time. Dab a small amount of glue onto one end of the wrapping ribbon, and place the glued end on the X on one ring. On the outside edge of the ring, use a push pin to attach one end of the decorative trim ribbon, and on the inside, use a pin to attach one end of the gold mesh. Leave a small end of each trim ribbon for gluing when you finish the last wrap.

8 Using the wrapping ribbon, wrap at a slight angle around the ring, leaving no cardboard showing. Alternate wrapping over or under the decorative and gold ribbon. Remember to wrap the rings the same way each time. Wrap evenly, adjusting the widths of the wrapping when you come to the end. Tuck in the ends of the ribbon on the underside, and glue. Repeat steps 7 and 8 for all rings.

9 Using the gold spray paint, spray two coats on both bases and the center oval you set aside in step 7. Paint both sides of each. Next, apply a coat of gold acrylic paint over the gold spray paint and allow to dry, then apply a coat of spray sealer. Allow to dry. Using glue, add decorative ribbon trim around the outside edges of both bases, and on the small raw edges of the center oval raw edges. Assemble your basket and enjoy!

TIPS: It is very important to remember how you wrapped each ring if you wish to keep the rings identical. You may want to alternate the gold to the outside, the decorative to the inside. If your ribbon is too thick, sandpaper the inner ledges of the base to accommodate the rings. For a totally different look, switch color schemes on the ring.

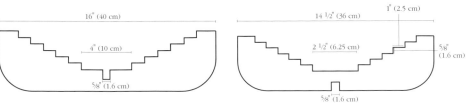

Fig. 3

Looping Memories

Loop your memories! Doris Messick shares her love of gathering little bits and pieces of nature on her travels. By using looping or knotless netting (an ancient basketry technique related to coiling), she turns her small collected treasures into a souvenir basket.

Designer: **DORIS MESSICK**

MATERIALS

Flexible vine

Waxed linen, choose a color that blends in with
the materials you are using

Spanish moss and/or other gathered materials

TOOLS

Pruning shears

#16 or #18 tapestry needle

Scissors

INSTRUCTIONS

1 Find a small vine, root, or
flexible branch to form a
framework for your basket.
Twist the vine around itself to
form an opening. This can be
any shape you prefer, from circular to free form; mine always
seem to become ovals.
(See figure 1.)

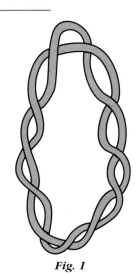

Fig. 1

2 With the remainder of
the vine, define the
outside shape of the basket.
Be sure all parts of the
framework have at least
two pieces of vine. More
than one vine can be used
if necessary. You can twist
them together or tie them
with the waxed linen
thread. (See figure 2).

Fig. 2

3 Using your waxed linen thread and tapestry needle, make a row of loops around one of the
pieces of vine at the rim, spacing the loops approximately ¼ inch (.6 cm) apart. To prevent the thread
from tangling, do not work with more than a 1-yard
(.9 m) length of thread at a time. Tie the linen onto
the rim leaving a 6 to 8-inch (15 to 20 cm) end dan-
gling for future use.

4 Following figure 3, go around one vine of the
frame and come through the resulting loop.
Repeat this step completely around the rim. Your
stitches can go either under or over the frame, and
either to the right or left. It is only necessary that
you go through the loop, which holds the stitch in
place—try different ways to see what is the easiest
for you.

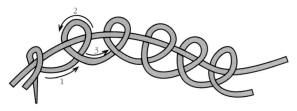

Fig. 3

5 The second row of looping loops onto the first, usually one stitch in every loop. If the space to be filled gets wider, add more loops by putting two loops into one on the previous row as needed. When the space becomes smaller, skip loops, doing one loop for every two from the previous row (figures 4, 5, and 6)

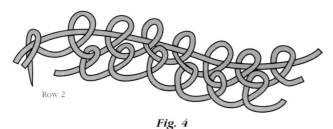

Row 2

Fig. 4

Increase

Fig. 5

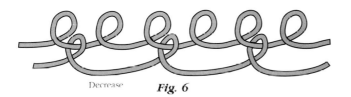

Decrease   **Fig. 6**

6 The third row of looping encloses the materials that you have gathered. Grasses or Spanish moss make a good base onto which other items can be added. Twist your gathering material into a manageable coil, and enclose it in your looping as shown in figure 7. Pull the waxed linen tight.

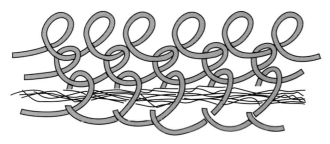

Fig. 7

7 From now on it will be difficult to see your stitches. Do not let that bother you. Just make sure the needle goes through a firm spot so it will not pull out. (If you can't see the stitches, no one else will, now you know why I like to use waxed linen thread that blends in.)

8 Shape the pouch as you go. Attach the loops to the side of framework in order to bring your looping down. This helps in forming the basket. Continue in this manner. Often you'll finish the front first; just continue to circle around with your looping until the basket is finished. Additional vine or ornamentation can be added at any time.

TIP: Looping can be used for many projects, either with or without enclosing other materials. You are limited only by your imagination. My favorite is a nest shape. As shown in the photo, I use dyed and painted egg gourds to complete the display.

Red Coiled Basket

Plastic tubing makes a versatile core for a coiled basket. You can use it as is, or try filling it with small beads before coiling for extra sparkle. This basket pairs tubing with plastic gimp for an easy-to-make design that's perfect for indoor or outdoor use.

Designer: **JOANNE WOOD PETERS**

MATERIALS

4-inch (10 cm) flexible plastic lid cover
¼-inch (.6 cm) clear plastic tubing, available in home-supply stores
Red gimp (plastic lacing) found in craft stores

TOOLS

Hole punch or awl
Scissors
Needle

INSTRUCTIONS

Finished dimensions: Base, 4 inches (10 cm); height, 2¾ inches (7 cm); rim diameter, 7 inches (17.5 cm)

1 Using the hole punch or awl, punch holes around the edge of the plastic lid, spacing the holes ¼ inch (.6 cm) apart. Using the scissors, taper one end of the plastic tubing, gradually trimming the taper back on the tubing for approximately 2½ to 3 inches (6.3 to 7.5 cm).

2 You will be coiling from the right side (the outside) of the basket, using a simple overhand stitch, also called a whip, plain, or rope stitch. Thread the needle with the gimp.

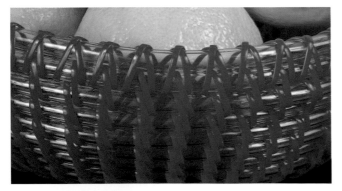

3 Place the tapered end of the tubing next to the edge of the plastic lid. You want the tapered end of the tubing to remain free, so start stitching approximately ⅛ inch (.3 cm) in from the end of the taper. Bring the gimp through a hole and up around the tubing. Coil the tubing around the edge of the lid, as you do, continue to lash the tubing to the edge by passing the gimp through each hole, then around the tubing.

4 When you've gone around the lid once, having returned to the tapered end, pass the gimp through a hole, then bring it around the taper and the tubing that is coiling on top of it. This completes the first row.

5 For the second row, continue the same overhand stitch, bringing the gimp around the first row of tubing, then around the second row. Continue in this way, coiling the tubing as you work, always passing the gimp first around the preceding coil, then around the outer coil.

6 Gradually shape the bowl out and up for approximately 12 rounds of coiling. To do this, place the new coil on top of and toward the outer edge of the coil preceding it. (See Shaping the Sides on page 95.)

7 You want to end your coiling at the same place you started. When you reach the location of the first taper, taper the end of the last coil. Lay the taper on the coiling and reverse your stitching, stitching to the left for one more round to create a border of crossed stitches. Secure the thread with a few overhand stitches around the last coil, then weave the gimp into the preceding stitches and coiling to hide the gimp before cutting the end.

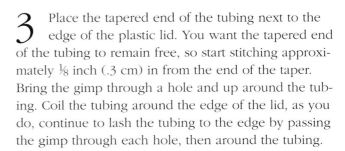

Mini Coiled Bolo Tie

Men love baskets too! Create this handsome tie using 26-gauge wire for the core and pearl cotton as the thread. By adding a pin back instead of attaching the cords, you could easily convert this bolo to a brooch.

Designer: **NICKI SHABAN**

MATERIALS

26-gauge floral wire (paddle wire) on a spool

Pearl cotton in red, black, and light silver metallic; used here, DMC #5 Coton Perle in red #999, black #310, and DMC #5 Perle Metalise in metallic pearl #5283

Leather or suede, approximately a 4-inch (10 cm) square

Black bolo cord, with metal back and tips

Black sewing thread

TOOLS

#1 embroidery needles

Small scissors (the smaller the better—cuticle scissors work well)

Small, flat-nose pliers

Small wire cutters

Strong, quick-drying glue (cyanoacrylate glue)

Sewing needle

INSTRUCTIONS

Finished dimensions: 2⅜ inches (6.7 cm) in diameter

1 From its spool, unravel approximately 12 inches (30 cm) of the 26-gauge wire. Do not cut it; it is easier to keep the wire on the spool while you work. Smooth all kinks from the wire.

2 Cut a 36-inch (.9 m) length of red pearl cotton, then thread one end through the embroidery needle. Lay the tail of thread next to the wire core. Starting ⅜ inch (.9 cm) in from the end of the wire (you want this end exposed, not wrapped), begin wrapping the thread around the core and tail as shown in figure 1.

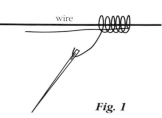

Fig. 1

3 Wrap for approximately ¼ inch (.6 cm). Then bend the wrapped wire so the beginning of the wrap meets the end of the wrap as shown in figure 2. This creates the center of the basket. The ⅜-inch (.9 cm) exposed end of the wire should now be lying against the core wire and the remaining unwrapped tail of thread. Continue to wrap all three pieces together with the red thread for approximately ⅛ inch (.3 cm) as shown in figure 3. Then bend this wrapped wire around the center to form a coil.

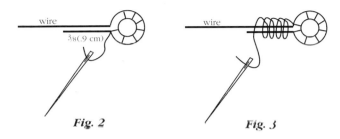

Fig. 2   **Fig. 3**

4 You will use the figure-eight stitch (see *Stitching the Coils* on page 94) to hold the center together. As shown in figure 4, wrap the thread

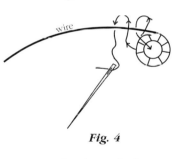

Fig. 4

around the top row, then bring it from the back to the front between the top wire and the center. Next, bring the thread through the center, then to the back of the basket again. You may find it helpful to use flat-nose pliers to pull the-needle through the center. Complete the figure-eight stitch by again bringing the thread from the back to the front between the top row and the bottom row. Continuing wrapping from right to left, using the pattern of two wraps followed by one figure-eight. As the basket gets larger, you can increase the wraps to three or four as needed.

5 You will need to add new thread when you run out, or when you are changing colors. Either way, plan on leaving a 3-inch (7.5 cm) tail of the old thread. Cut another 36-inch (.9 m) length of thread, threading it onto another needle. Lay the tail of the new length next to your core materials, and continue the pattern around the new thread. When the new

thread has been covered for approximately ½ inch (1.3 cm), remove the needle from the old thread, letting the remaining tail become a part of the core, and begin wrapping with the new thread.

6 The bolo shown follows this pattern:

Row 1: Center in red

Row 2: Red, two wraps to one figure-eight

Row 3: Red, three wraps to one figure-eight

Row 4: Black and red, four black wraps to two red figure-eights

Row 5: Metallic, metallic wraps and metallic figure-eights (place the metallic figure-eight stitches at the beginning and end of the black sections on previous row.)

Rows 6 and 7: Metallic, three wraps to one figure-eight

Rows 8 and 9: Black, three wraps to one figure-eight

Rows 10 and 11: Red, three wraps to one figure-eight

Rows 12 and 13: Metallic, three wraps to one figure-eight

Rows 14 and 15: Black, three wraps to one figure-eight (row 15 is the rim of the miniature basket)

7 At the end of the 15th row, cut the 26-gauge wire from the spool, leaving a ¼ inch (.6 cm) tail. Do not cut the black thread. To hide the end of the wire, wrap the black thread around the 15th row (rim) and the end of the wire until the end is incorporated into the rim. On the back side of the basket, use a sewing needle to run the end of the black thread under previous stitches, then cut the thread.

8 Cut a circle of leather slightly smaller than the basket. Sew and glue the metal bolo back to center of this circle. Using a sewing needle and thread, attach the leather circle to the back of basket. Slip the basket onto the bolo cords, then glue the bolo tips to the ends of the cords.

TIP: Clean all tools before starting the basket to prevent any grease or residue from rubbing onto the thread.

Red Hot Chili Pepper

You will use almost every part of the gourd to make this basket. The hanging embellishments are large gourd seeds—when dyed red, they resemble chili peppers. Fill the finished gourd with bottles of homemade salsa and packages of chili spices for a memorable gift basket.

Designer: **DYAN KNITTLE**

MATERIALS

Gourd
Gourd seeds
Leather dye, paint, or shoe polish
Clear acrylic spray
Paper towels
¼-inch (.6 cm) sisal rope
Waxed linen thread

TOOLS

Small saw
Grapefruit spoon
Sandpaper, 150 grit
Tape measure
Pencil and eraser
Awl, or small drill with a ⅛-inch (.3 cm) drill bit
Paintbrush, disposable sponge brushes work well
Craft knife
Darning or tapestry needle
Pliers

INSTRUCTIONS

1 Using the saw, cut off the top of the gourd. Using the grapefruit spoon, clean out the inside of the gourd. Reserve the seeds, wash them thoroughly, then place them on paper towels and set them aside to dry. Use 150-grit sandpaper to smooth the inside and outside of the gourd.

2 To determine how many gourd seeds you will need, and as a guide for making the holes, mark the outside of the gourd. Using a pencil, position the marks ¼ inch (.6 cm) down from the top of the gourd, spacing the marks ½ to 1 inch (1.3 to 2.5 cm) apart around the gourd. Using the awl or drill, punch or drill holes in the gourd, then in the top part of the seeds. Erase any pencil marks.

3 Using the shoe dye, paint, or shoe polish, and a paintbrush, paint the inside and outside of the gourd and the seeds. Allow to dry for several hours or overnight. Spray the inside and outside of the gourd and the seeds with clear acrylic spray. Allow to dry for a few hours.

4 Using the craft knife, cut one end of the rope at an angle. (This will give a nice flowing start to the coil.) Thread your needle with waxed linen thread. Lay the angled end of the rope on the rim of the gourd. To attach the rope, start from the inside of the gourd and take the thread through a hole and string on a seed. Then go up and over the rope, encircling the rope. Next take the thread through the same holes (gourd and seed) again. Your stitch should look like a V. Continue coiling and stitching in this way around the rim.

5 Before you begin your next row, stitch backwards (backstitch), taking one stitch in each seed hole all the way around to the starting point. Your stitches will look like an arrow. If you need to end a thread and start a new one, weave the ends in and out to hide them.

6 Start the second row. Instead of stitching through the holes as in step 4, you will stitch through the middle of the rope, and through the center of the arrow stitch. You may need to use the pliers to help you pull the needle through the rope. Before beginning the third row, as you did in step 5, backstitch to form your arrow.

7 Repeat step 6 for four or five rows, or more if you desire. End by finishing the coil at the same place you started, cutting the rope on an angle as you did in step 4; this will blend the end and the coil together.

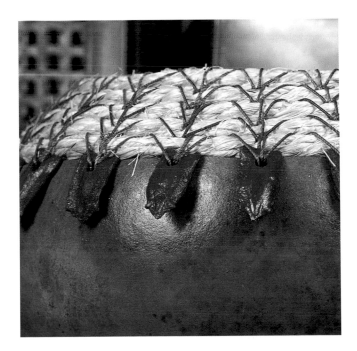

Black Thorn Gourd

Designer Judy Mallow used the limbs of Poncirus, or black thorn, to create this dramatic gourd basket. The thorns of Poncirus are very sharp, and you will need to use caution when handling them. You can modify this design by using any vine to embellish the top of the gourd.

Designer: **JUDY MOFIELD MALLOW**

MATERIALS

Bushel gourd (a large-variety gourd)
Leather dye or paint
Pine needles
24- and 28-gauge copper wire
Poncirus (black thorn) limbs
Black fabric dye

TOOLS

Small saw or motorized craft tool with
  a cutting blade
Drill, or motorized craft tool, and
  small drill bit
Wood-burning tool (optional)
Sewing needle
Scissors
Pruning shears
Needle-nose pliers

INSTRUCTIONS

Note: Use extreme caution with the thorns of *Poncirus trifoliate orange*! They are very sharp. I recommend using a pair of leather work gloves when handling them. When dyeing them, use tongs to manipulate them in and out of the dye bath.

1 Using the saw, cut the top off of the gourd. Clean out the inside membrane and pulp. Using the drill, drill holes around the top edge of the gourd.

2 Decorate the outside of the gourd as desired. You can dye, paint, carve, or wood burn it. This gourd has a copper metallic finish.

3 Using 24-gauge copper wire, sew clusters of four pine needles around the top edge of the gourd. You may find it helpful to thread the wire on a needle. Pass the wire through the holes in the gourd, and encircle the clusters to secure them. Add a new cluster of pine needles every four or five holes. To keep the coil of pine needles uniform, trim some of the pine-needle coil that's already on the gourd when you add a new cluster.

4 Prepare the Poncirus limbs by cutting all side shoots, leaving only thorns. Using fabric dye, dye the Poncirus until it is a deep black. Allow to dry.

5 Using the 28-gauge wire, sew the limbs to the pine-needle coil. Decoratively wrap sections of the limbs and thorns as you go, attaching the limbs occasionally to the pine-needle coil. Use the needle-nose pliers to help you wrap the limbs and thorns. Add additional limbs if desired on top of the first row. I used two rows for this design.

6 The base for the basket is made from two branches of Poncirus. Circle a branch and secure it with a wrapping of wire. Repeat for the other branch. Lay the two circular bases on top of each other, arranging them to fit the bottom of the gourd.

109

Genie-Jar or Wishing-Jar Basket

Children can easily make these simple
baskets to give as special gifts. As well as
holding wishes or dreams, the baskets can hold special or cherished objects,
and can be embellished with drawings or meaningful trinkets. All supplies
are readily available, making a trip to your local hardware store, craft-sup-
ply store, and bead shop a fun outing for you and your child.

Designer: **HELEN FROST WAY**

MATERIALS

Cotton clothesline, or any smooth, large,
   natural-fiber cording
Small ball, tennis-ball size or larger
Assorted fun papers or cut-out pictures
   from magazines
Acrylic gloss medium
Acrylic paints
Crayons and colored pencils
Assorted trinkets, such as buttons, ribbons, glitter,
   little animals, flowers, corks, feathers, etc.
String, yarn, or heavy thread

TOOLS

Hot glue gun and glue sticks
Scissors
Paintbrushes

INSTRUCTIONS

Note: Hot glue and glue guns are very hot. Adult
help is recommended for the first four steps and
when gluing on trinkets.

1 Make the base of the basket. Coil the clothesline
   into a flat, tight circle (approximately four or five
turns). Hold the line in this shape and glue, placing
the glue in the spaces between the coils. (The glue
will seep into the fibers.) Continue holding the shape
until the glue sets. Do not cut the clothesline.

2 Place the glued base on top of the ball and hold it
   there. Now slowly begin to coil the line around
the ball. Coil approximately 1 inch (2.5 cm) at a time,
gluing the coils to each other as you go; it will become
easier as you get farther along. Continue coiling and gluing up to the halfway mark on your ball form.

3 Now pull the ball out, and proceed to coil and
   glue the rest of the way. You will now be working without a form. As with coiling, you will be
decreasing to shape the basket. To decrease, place
each row of coiling slightly to the inside of the previous coil, then glue. Shape the top of the basket to
look like the bottom. Stop when you have reached the
point where you would like to have a stopper or lid.
Allow time for the glue to dry. Check for areas you
have missed, filling in with additional glue at this time.

4 You may make a fancy stopper or a lid. To make
   a stopper, coil almost all the way to the top and
leave a hole for your stopper. To make a lid, coil a
separate flat circle as you did for the base, or coil a
curved lid by again using your form. Make stoppers
from wooden pegs or corks. Hinge lids on one side by
piercing holes in the lid and the basket, then thread
string, yarn, or thread through the holes to tie the two
together. To make the project very simple, you may
omit the stopper or lid, and make a bowl by only coiling halfway up your form.

5 Now that your basket is formed, paint it, and/or
   adhere fun papers. Glue papers using acrylic
gloss medium; simply lay the papers on the basket
and paint over them with the medium. Allow the project to dry thoroughly, then glue on desired objects or
embellish the surface with your own drawings.

Joyful Coils

You can find all the materials for this vibrant vessel at a hardware or home-supply store. Designer Mary Robinson says, "I believe you should choose your own colors, so I will not tell you which to use. However, I strongly suggest a random selection—that is what makes this vessel so joyful for me."

Designer: **MARY ROBINSON**

MATERIALS

Cotton clothesline, do not use vinyl or plastic
Multi-use nylon twine, used here in lime green, bright yellow, neon pink, orange, and gold.
10 copper pipe clamps
54 to 72 inches (1.4 to 1.8 m) of 24-gauge copper wire

TOOLS

Scissors
Darning or tapestry needle, the eye must be large enough for the nylon twine

INSTRUCTIONS

Note: If you are a beginner, I suggest you practice the following coiling techniques using acrylic yarn over clothesline before working with the nylon twine.

1 You will leave the clothesline in one piece, but cut the nylon twine into lengths, each approximately 2 yards (1.8 m) long. Cut the nylon as you need it, since the twine tends to fray when cut.

2 Thread the needle with a length of twine in a color of your choice. Following figure 1, secure the tail of the twine by laying it along the clothesline, then tightly wrap the twine over the core and tail for 1½ inches (3.8 cm).

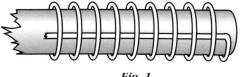

Fig. 1

3 Fold the core in on itself, making a small, tight circle. Following figure 2, hold the circle while you use a few overhand loops to bind the coiled end of the rope to itself. Following figure 3, begin a figure-eight stitch to secure the circle. If you need to add a new piece of twine, use the same technique as in step 2, covering the old tail as well as the new tail.

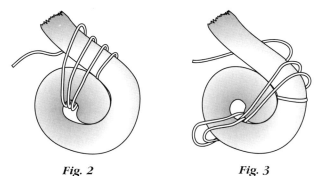

Fig. 2   ***Fig. 3***

4 Each coil is fastened to the previous coil with the figure-eight stitch (see Stitching the Coils, page 94). I really like this stitch because it provides texture and color variation. For this basket, wrap the core four to five times, then make a figure-eight stitch. Continue this sequence as you coil, being careful to make your wrapping and stitches as even as possible. Alternate colors as desired until you've coiled a circle with a 4-½-inch (11.3 cm) diameter.

5 Begin to increase the diameter of the vessel with each row until the side of the vessel is approximately 2 inches (5 cm) high, and is approximately 6 to 6½ inches (15 to 16.3 cm) in diameter. Then work two rows without increasing by placing the new coil directly on top of the previous coil, changing colors as

desired. Note: As you coil the sides, you will be increasing (building out and up) and decreasing (building in and up) to shape your vessel. You will be building the sides at a gentle curve, not a right angle. To do this, always hold the new coil in the position you want the vessel to grow, placing the core on the previous coil either to the outside of the coil for increasing, or to the inside for decreasing.

6 Start your decrease, placing the coil so each row curves gently inward. Keep decreasing until the vessel measures 3½ inches (8.8 cm) high and approximately 5 to 5½ inches (12.5 to 13.8 cm) in diameter.

7 Attach the pipe clamps. You want to do this while the mouth of the vessel is still wide enough to accommodate your hand. You will attach the clamps by their top holes first. Coil the next row, treating the top hole of the pipe clamp as part of the core by looping the twine around the core and through the clamp's hole, as shown in figure 4. Space the clamps approximately 1 inch (2.5 cm) apart. Leave a space of approximately 2½ inches (6.25) between the first and last clamp for connecting the handle. When the row is completed and all the clamps are in the coil, use three stitches in each bottom hole to attach the clamps to the lower coil.

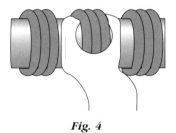

Fig. 4

8. Once the clamps are attached, continue decreasing for another 1 inch (2.5 cm) until the vessel is approximately 3 to 3½ inches (7.5 to 8.8 cm) in diameter. Begin making the neck and lip. For the neck, work one row without increasing or decreasing. Identify the center point of the vessel, which is directly opposite the center of the space you left between the first and last clamp. On the next row, approximately ½ inch (1.3 cm) from this center point, wrap approximately 1¼ inches (3 cm) of core. Ease this section into a 1-inch (2.5 cm) space, centering the wrapping on either side of the center point, then attach it with a figure-eight stitch; this makes the lip. Continue working around the vessel until you are within ¼ inch (.6 cm) of the center point on the opposite side of the vessel, which will be the handle side.

9 To make the handle, wrap a 3½-inch (8.8 cm) section of the core with nylon twine. Attach this wrapped section to the vessel by stitching it to the eighth row of coiling from the top. Wrap another 3½-inch (8.8 cm) section of core, and loop it up toward the top, attaching it to the top of the vessel by continuing to coil the next row.

10 Coil to the side opposite the handle, stopping at the same center point where you worked the increase for the lip. Wrap 1½ inches (3.8 cm) of core, and as you did in step 8, ease the wrapped section into a 1¼-inch (3 cm) space. Continue coiling until you get back to the handle.

11 Cut the clothesline core and nylon twine leaving a 1-inch (2.5 cm) tail. Place the tails on top of the handle. Wrap nylon twine around the tails of the core and twine to hide them, while at the same time binding them to the top of the handle. To secure the binding, use a needle to thread the end of the binding twine through the wrapping several times before cutting the end.

12 To finish, make the tassels which will hang from the bottom of the copper clamps. For each tassel, cut a 2-yard (1.8 m) length of nylon twine, and thread it through your needle. Push the needle crosswise through the three stitches that attach the bottom of the copper clamp to the vessel. Make a 3-inch (7.5 cm) loop, sewing back through the stitches, then repeat, leaving a 3-inch (7.5 cm) loop each time. Continue looping until you've used the length of twine.

13 Cut a 4-inch (10 cm) piece of wire. Wrap it around the top of the tassel and twist tightly, with the twisted ends toward the vessel. Push the ends of the wire through the coil, and open the ends on the inside to secure. Cut the bottoms of the twine loops, separating the strands to fluff the tassel. Trim the bottom of each tassel, making the ends even with the bottom of the vessel. If desired, you can make a large tassel from all the twine colors to hang from the handle. Make the tassel approximately 3 inches (7.5 cm) long. Use the wire to wrap the tassel numerous times, then tie the tassel to the bottom of the handle. Do not separate the strands.

Artist's Statement
Rob Dobson

The work of Rob Dobson of Bedford, Massachusetts, is a perfect example of new basketry that combines an innovative use of material with an energetic understanding of form. By sharing this statement, he provides insight into his vision for working with nontraditional materials.

I have a passion for applying traditional fiber techniques to nontraditional materials. I see my sculptural weaving as an art of inclusion, and I work with an extremely broad definition of "fiber." Just about anything flexible becomes fair game in this effort to gather and interlace the great breadth of stuff in the world.

For me, weaving is an art of assemblage and juxtaposition; the satisfaction lies in making an inventive whole out of disparate parts. In all of the collecting and joining and

Basket #34, 1998, 7" x 14" x 12" (17.5 x 35 x 30 cm); plainweave, twined, strung, assembled; twigs, electrical wire, plastic pipe, wooden beads from car backrest, plastic wire nuts. Photo by Jeff Baird

overlapping, I find that the outer work of weaving mirrors the disciplined inner weaving an examined life requires for integrity and wholeness. In Tantric philosophy the root word tan means to weave.

Because of my longstanding interest in discovering value in the discarded, I work almost exclusively with materials I salvage from my surroundings. These raw found elements have their own characteristics that can push a work in unexpected directions. I shop for my materials at dumpsters all over Boston, at the beach, in the woods. Shiny things and dull things, supple and stiff, metal, wood, plastic, weathered, brand-new, in this search nothing is left out. In the most basic way, my work springs out of my community and my environment.

Salvaged materials first revealed their virtues to me when I was making my living as a weaver in Arizona in the 1970s. With a limited cash flow for yarn, I expanded on traditional rag rug techniques by cutting up thrift store winter coats (abundant and cheap in Tucson) to make beautiful wool strips for weft. Occasionally needing a change of

Basket #9, 1995, 12" x 27½" x 3½" (30 x 70 x 8.8 cm); twined and assembled; steel pallet strapping, electrical wire, plastic wire nuts, PVC pipe, wood, miscellaneous fasteners. Photo by Dean Powell

pace from the loom, I started to experiment with sculptural baskets, constructing the first ones from fabric strips woven onto date palm stems.

These days, in the midst of our culture's rush toward the disembodied world of cyberspace, I find myself still choosing consciously to spend a good deal of my time participating in the tangible, funky world, to grapple playfully with unwieldy lengths of this and that. It is visual art, but it is about the hands as well as the eyes, about hammers and tinsnips and needle-nose pliers. Modern as it is in some ways, my work also harks back to the kind of dignity and pride that were possible for a craftsperson before the Industrial Revolution's mass production methods obscured individual skill and ingenuity.

JONI BAMFORD, *Lidded Basket*, 1998, 9" x 9" (22.5 x 22.5 cm); bias plaiting starting from a bias corner; metal hoops, paper, mirror tape. Photo by Evan Bracken

JOANNA GILMOUR, *Pointed Casket*, 1998, 5¾" x 4¾" (14 x 12 cm); bias plaiting; decorated watercolor paper, bamboo, plastic coated wire. Photo by V. Gilmour

MARY LEE FULKERSON, *Unraveling the Basket: Gathering Her Fragments*, 1999, 46" x 60" x 5" (117 x 150 x 12.5 cm); twining, collage, wrapping; coated wire spokes, reed, neckties, paper clay, willow, bark shavings, beads, fetishes, paint.
Photo courtesy of the artist

JAMES T. RICHARDSON, *Vessel #184*, 1999, 23" x 17" x 15" (58.5 x 42.5 x 37.5 cm); coiled, banded with copper strips, soldered, wrapped, painted; copper tubing, sheet copper, copper wire. Photo by Jerry Anthony

MICHAEL DAVIS, *Medieval Pine Cone II*, 1995, 24" x 14" x 14" (61 x 35 x 35 cm); twining, stitching; painted pine cone petals, reed, acrylic and enamel paint. Photo by Deloye Burrell

JACKIE ABRAMS, *Hexagonal Weave #39*, 1998, 6" x 8" x 8" (15 x 20 x 20 cm); hexagonal weave with two layers of interlacing; watercolor paper, paint, waxed linen, varnish. Photo by Jeff Baird

CAROL STANGLER, *Hornets' Nest in Winter*, 1999, 36" x 30" x 12" (91.5 x 76 x 30 cm); random weave; sweetgum branch, muscadine and kudzu vines, hemlock and birch bark, dyed reed, and hornets' nest fragments. Photo by Evan Bracken

DEBRA SACHS, *Blue Buoy*, 1997, 25" x 12½" x 12½" (63.5 x 31 x 31 cm); weaving; wood, copper refrigeration tubing, paper twine, copper wire, mixed polymers. Photo by the artist

ANDREA DUFLON, *Navarro*, 1998, 6" x 9" x 9" (15 x 22.5 x 22.5); coiling; horsetail, driftwood, waxed linen, Photo by Kate Cameron

VICKI JOHNSON, *Miniature copper and silver egg baskets*, 1999, 1" x ³⁄₄" x ³⁄₄" (2.5 x 1.9 x 1.9 cm); woven with ribbed construction; 28- to 18-gauge copper and silver wire. Photo by Evan Bracken

ZOE MORROW, *Token + Twigs*, 1999, 7" x 8" x 3" (17.5 x 20 x 7.5 cm); wrapping and weaving (plain weave), formed and stiffened; shredded money (printing rejects), twigs, old tax token. Photo by C. Jenkins III

HELEN FROST WAY, Grouping, L. to R. *Dig #1 - Site #2, Dig #1 - Site #1, Maze #2, Dig #1 - Site #3*, 1999, 6¼" x 5³⁄₄" (16 x 14.5 cm), 8" x 6¼" (20 x 16 cm), 6¼" x 12" (16 x 30 cm), 8" x 6¼" (20 x 16 cm); coiling; mixed media. Photo courtesy of the artist

LaVerne Theis, *Current Event*, 1999, 8" x 20" (20 x 50 cm); twining, Japanese spiral, three-rod wale, and English randing; electrical wire, y-connectors, willow, wild rose, seagrass. Photo by Evan Bracken

Polly Harrison, *Tired Old Dog*, 1996, 17" x 8" x 8" (42.5 x 20 x 20 cm); twining over wire armature; auto inner tubes, wire, wooden rings, chain, dog tags. Photo by the artist

Patti Quinn Hill, *Venus in Blue Jeans*, 1999, 18" x 24" (45 x 61 cm); twill weave; cotton archival paper, acrylic paint, rattan, waxed linen. Photo by the artist

Emily Dvorin, *Moodish Blues*, 1998, 7" x 18" (17.5 x 45 cm); coiling; rolled paper, waxed cord, beads, peacock feathers. Photo by B. Kamin

Billie Ruth Sudduth, *The Sunday Paper*, 1993, 10" x 17" x 10" (25 x 42.5 x 25 cm); plaiting, weaving; newspaper, dyed reed splint. Photo courtesy of the artist

Barbara Compton, *Umbrella Basket*, 1996, 27" x 24" x 32" (68.5 x 61 x 81.5 cm); plaiting, twining, stitching; cardboard, procion-dyed reed, nylon twine, wallpaper tubes, hot glue, latex paint, varnish. Photo courtesy of the Art Museum of Missoula, Montana

Marilyn Sharp, *Billie's Basket*, 1999, 8" x 13" x 13" (20 x 32.5 x 32.5 cm); twining; paper rush, waxed thread, curved bone bead. Photo by R. Sharp

DEB CURTIS, *Swirl*, 1997, 8" x 9" (20 x 22.5 cm); twining; seagrass, paper made from iris leaves and philodendron sheath, buttons, beads. Photo by the artist

DYAN MAI PETERSON, *Gourd basket*, 1999, 18" x 15" (45 x 37.5 cm); coiling, braided handle; gourd, pine needles, waxed linen, beads. Photo by Evan Bracken

JOANNE WOOD PETERS, *Antler bowl*, 1999, 8" x 12" x 5" (20 x 30 x 12.5 cm); twining; antler, telephone wire, raffia, hemp, seagrass, yarn, rayon cord, leather cord, chenille, sisal. Photo by Evan Bracken

JUDY MALLOW, *Fran's Basket*, 1998, 3½" x 6" x 3½" (8.8 x 15 x 8.8 cm); coiling; dyed long leaf pine needles (unnaturally bent during a hurricane). Photo by Don McKenzie

GAIL CAMPBELL, *Vessel #351*, 1998, 26¼" x 13¼" x 13" (67 x 35 x 33 cm); weaving, twining, tapestry techniques; white pine bark, patinated copper strips, copper wire, raffia, waxed linen thread, Czechoslovakian glass beads. Photo by Jerry Anthony

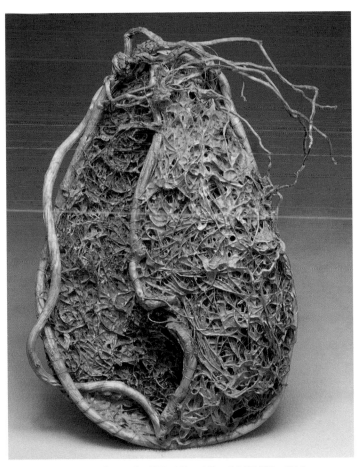

DORIS MESSICK, *For the Birds*, 1999, 18" x 11" x 4-1/2" (45 x 27.5 x 11.3 cm); random weave dipped in paper pulp; recycled brass wire, honeysuckle vine, paper pulp, paint. Photo by the artist

Contributing Designers

JACKIE ABRAMS explores both traditional and contemporary basket techniques, creating her own materials with paper and paint. She experiments with interactions and combinations of color, texture, and form, finding the possibilities "endless and exciting!" Jackie lives in Topsham, Vermont.

JODI BAMFORD of Empingham, England, teaches basketmaking and off-loom weaving, specializing in plaiting and hexagonal open weave. As a dedicated environmental campaigner, she likes to use recyclable materials, such as plastic packing tape and paper, as well as prunings from hedgerows and gardens.

DEB CURTIS of Corvallis, Oregon, combines traditional basket weaving with handmade paper, beading, stitching, and surface design. Designs for her baskets come from objects found in the natural world or from the feelings that emerge while creating the basket. She strives to show that there is beauty in tradition and purpose to contemporary basketry.

PEGGY DEBELL admits this is the first basket she has ever made! Peggy is a fiber artist, making hand-painted/printed clothing and mixed media wall pieces. According to Peggy, Patti Hill, whom she credits as a "real basketmaker," helped her put this one together. Peggy lives and works in Asheville, North Carolina, and is member of the Southern Highlands Craft Guild.

MARY LEE FULKERSON exhibits in museums and galleries as well as being part of many corporate collections. She is the founder of Great Basin Basketmakers and the author of *Weavers of Tradition and Beauty*, published by University of Nevada Press. A smaller version of her basket on page 64 was selected for the 1999 White House Christmas tree. Mary lives in Reno, Nevada.

LYNN B. GAMMON of Houston, Texas, has been profiled in national publications, and has had her work featured in numerous galleries and exhibitions. She says her art creates in her a sense of quiet and purpose, and, if it causes the same reaction in the people viewing it, she is fulfilled.

MOLLY GARDNER feels that baskets are timeless vessels that have survived through the ages as part of our heritage and history. Some of her baskets are utilitarian, but she gets the most enjoyment from creating unique and decorative pieces. Molly, who lives in Sun Valley, Nevada, also enjoys teaching basketmaking workshops and working with other basketmakers through guilds.

POLLY HARRISON shows her concern for the depletion of the earth's resources by transforming discarded materials into baskets using traditional techniques. She conducts artist-in-residence programs with the Georgia Council for the Arts and the South Carolina Arts Commission. Polly has participated in exhibits world wide, and is represented by The Signature Shop in Atlanta, Georgia.

VICKI JOHNSON, who started weaving in 1994, considers herself a traditional, functional basketmaker. She is particularly intrigued by the grace, beauty, and function of the Appalachian egg basket. Vicki lives in Sparks, Nevada, where she currently enjoys staying at home with her two children, and weaving baskets as often as she can.

KAREN KAUSHANSKY of Seattle, Washington, enjoys creating baskets using a multitude of materials and styles. Her work has been shown in group shows, gallery exhibits, and craft fairs. She continuously experiments with her work, and specializes in making baskets for individuals that reflect a personal story, using various materials to weave the story into the work.

DYAN KNITTLE is a self-taught basketmaker who enjoys expanding her knowledge through books, involvement in guilds, and hands-on projects. She brings her passion for nature to her work by using a variety of plant materials in her baskets. Her main focus is pine-needle basketry, but she also loves to experiment with other fibers. Dyan lives in Reno Nevada.

NANCY MCGAHA enjoys experimenting with mixing media and craft techniques. She works in a variety of crafts, particularly beadwork—both loomed and peyote stitch—as well as rigid-heddle loom weaving, and creating fiber-art wall hangings.

Contributing Designers

JUDY MOFIELD MALLOW is a fifth-generation basketmaker, and author of two books on pine needle basketry. She owns and operates Prim Pines in Carthage, North Carolina, a mail-order business that provides pine-needle basket supplies nationwide. Currently Judy is teaching workshops at the John C. Campbell Folk School in Brasstown, North Carolina.

DORIS MESSICK is a contemporary basketmaker, teacher, and writer from the Eastern Shore of Maryland, who specializes in the use of natural materials which she has grown or gathered from the wild. Doris has exhibited and taught nationally since 1982, enjoying the opportunity to travel, meet new people, and see the wonderful materials unique to each area.

JOANNE WOOD PETERS has a lifetime of experience in various fiber arts, but is currently centering on basket weaving. She especially enjoys developing new designs, writing patterns for them, then teaching them at basketry conventions nationwide. Joanne, from Holyoke, Massachusetts, sells her baskets in galleries in New England and the Midwest.

DYAN MAI PETERSON is multi-talented designer, basketmaker, and gourd artist who never seems to run out of ideas. She applies her wide-ranging talents to her gourd business while also teaching gourd craft and basketry. She is a member of the Southern Highlands Craft Guild, living and working in Asheville, North Carolina.

LINDA RAGSDALE is a designer and manufacturer of triple-walled cardboard furniture, frames, and home accents. She works with her sister under their business name "Mixed Nuts." Her work has been featured on nationally-broadcast TV craft shows and in numerous publications. She lives and works outside of Nashville, in Old Hickory, Tennessee. You can reach her via e-mail at mixednuts@mindspring.com

MARY A. ROBINSON graduated from the University of Kentucky with a BA in studio art with an emphasis in fiber. She has been a member of the Lexington Fiber Guild for four years and has exhibited with them. She is currently working on her "Women of the Bible" series. Mary lives in Lexington Kentucky.

NICKI SHABAN of Braintree, Massachusetts, first learned basketry through an adult education program. She now focuses on creating wearable works of art. Her basket patterns and kits can be found in basketry supply stores and on internet web sites. Nicki is a member of both The Northeast and Lexington Arts and Crafts Society Basketmakers Guilds and enjoys teaching workshops for them. You can reach Nicki at kshaban@ibm.net

SHEILA SHEPPARD is a full-time multimedia studio artist from Jonesborough, Tennessee, who works in polymer, wood, metals, and found objects. She holds workshops that seek to be an exploration of the creative spirit. Her favorite artists are her children and grandchildren.

CAROL STANGLER is an environmental artist and weaver who creates baskets and sculpture from vines, bark, grasses, and other natural materials. She teaches extensively and exhibits her work in Atlanta, Georgia, and throughout the Southeast. She lives and works in Asheville, North Carolina.

LINDA ARTER SURA of Slidell, Louisiana, enjoys creating one-of-a-kind pieces, and hopes to find enough time to weave all the baskets she imagines. She has been experimenting with contemporary styles for a number of years, and is an award-winning basketmaker and teacher.

HELEN FROST WAY shows her work nationally, lectures, teaches, and curates shows. She is the founder/director of The Firehouse Gallery in Damariscotta, Maine, which showcases fine contemporary American crafts by leading artists.

SYLVIA WHITE has been making fiber containers for thirty years. Her interest in baskets began from living in Africa during the 1960s and 70s. Currently, she is experimenting with recycled and new man-made materials. Sylvia teaches basketry and is a member of Franklin House Gallery in Port Townsend, Washington

Glossary

Base + Height + Height: Formula used to determine the measurement for the stakes and spokes.

Chase Weave: Use of two weavers over an even number of stakes or spokes. One weaver follows the other, "chasing" it around the stakes or spokes.

Coiling: Spiraling and stitching together a round core element.

Continuous Weave: Use of one weaver over an odd number of stakes or spokes.

Core: The spiraling element in coiling. The core can be a single-element core, or can be composed of thinner individual elements grouped together to form a single core.

Diagonal/Bias Plaiting: Plaiting by weaving the elements at right angles to each other.

False Rim: The last row of weaving.

Four-Rod Wale: In twining, weaving four separate weavers in sequence either over three stakes and under one, or over two stakes and under two.

Hexagonal Plaiting: An open weave created by weaving the elements into a series of interlocking hexagonals.

Lasher: The element that lashes the rim to the basket.

Pair Twining: Using two weavers when twining.

Plain Weave: Passing the weaver over the stakes or spokes in an over one, under one pattern.

Plaiting: Weaving like elements together.

Rim: An applied rim, usually composed of two strips positioned over the false rim, then lashed in placed using a simple overhand stitch.

Spokes: Terminology for stakes in a round basket.

Stakes: The elements that first compose the woven base, then, when turned upright, become the upright elements.

Stop-Start Weave: The use of a separate weaver for each row, worked over an even number of stakes.

Straight Plaiting: Plaiting by passing weavers horizontally or vertically over the stakes.

Three-Rod Wale: In twining, weaving three separate weavers in sequence over two stakes and under one.

Track Border: In twining, bending the stakes over in sequence to create a finished rim.

True the Base: To adjust the woven base elements before turning the elements upright. Truing ensures that all the corners are square and all the ends are an equal length.

Twill: Weaving over two, under two for a balanced twill, or over three, under one for an unbalanced twill.

Twining: Using two or more weavers to encircle the stakes or spokes.

Visible Core: In coiling, placing the stitches apart, allowing the core element to be visible.

Waling: Using three or more weavers when twining.

Weaver: The element that is woven around the stakes or spokes to create the weave.

Weaving: Passing a weaver over and under the stakes or spokes.

Wrapped Core: In coiling, placing the stitches close together or wrapping the core to completely cover the core element.